D0964497

Eldridge Cleaver
REBORN

Eldridge Cleaver
REBORN

by
John A. Oliver

Logos International
Plainfield, New Jersey

ELDRIDGE CLEAVER: REBORN
Copyright © 1977 by Logos International
All rights reserved
Printed in the United States of America
International Standard Book Number: 0-88270-233-5 (paper)
Library of Congress catalog card number: 77-74797
Published by Logos International
Plainfield, New Jersey 07061

CONTENTS

PROLOGUE

Tension and impatience heightened the usual busy excitement of Kennedy International Airport the afternoon of November 18, 1975, for those who awaited the arrival of TWA Flight 803 from Paris.

The high-security daily diplomatic flight between France and the United States had been delayed by a runway blockage in Paris and was more than three hours late. So the trim-suited, tight-lipped FBI agents stood or sat, or paced and smoked. Watching them from the inner corridor in which they were restricted from the field entrance to the airport building, a hundred or so newsmen and TV cameramen idled around, chatting, fussing with equipment, speculating. Both groups were taut and expectant. The diplomatic flight always carried important personages who required security and news coverage. Especially today.

On the delayed flight, a big, lithe, black man, in a dark jacket and white turtleneck, sat with two companions. From time to time they all chatted, breaking the longer periods of silence that kept settling, grabbing their individual thoughts.

As the plane approached the airport, the big black man and his companions put on seat belts for landing as did all the passengers.

At the airport, when the flight was announced, the tension in the two groups clustered around the arrival gate loosened, and an eagerness set in. The trim-suited FBI agents closed ranks, newsmen jostled and jockeyed for position.

Touchdown brought the familiar brief screech of tire-skid. The plane taxied in, and the passenger hatch opened a black hole in the jet's side. Stooping to let his six-foot-two frame through, the big black man, now wearing a black raincoat, descended toward the waiting agents and their handcuffs. Ex-con Eldridge Cleaver, former minister of information for the Black Panther Party, parole escapee and federal fugitive was home at last from his self-imposed seven-year exile. Most notable, he had come home voluntarily.

His return is a commentary on America's times and national character.

Wedging him in their midst, the FBI men hustled Cleaver through customs to the airport's federal building to be fingerprinted and photographed. Cleaver, sweating beneath television lights and looking apprehensive as newsmen crowded about, turned aside the obvious questions.

"It's ridiculous to ask me questions in these circumstances," he said. "I came back because I wanted to."

His comments continued to be short, almost curt, as reporters and photographers followed him into the corridors and en route to the Federal District Court in

Brooklyn where Cleaver was arraigned. In a small, crowded courtroom he was charged with unlawful flight to escape prosecution. It took an hour and a half before United States Magistrate Vincent A. Catoggio and Cleaver's attorneys, Napoleon B. Williams and Lennox Hinds of Manhattan worked out all the details. The federal prosecutor asked for $100,000 bail; Cleaver's attorneys objected to that, the handcuffs and the surrounding marshals. Eldridge Cleaver had returned voluntarily, they said. Finally Cleaver was placed overnight in a courthouse jail, to await flight the next morning to California in the custody of Bureau of Prison marshals. It would be up to them whether he was handcuffed or not.

Cleaver's return had been expected for weeks prior to his actual arrival. Even before his arrival he had come under much criticism and suspicion. He was a contradiction, an anomaly, an anachronism, as if, wrote Wallace Turner in a side-bar story from San Francisco for the *New York Times*, " . . . the mastodon had walked out of the glacier's face, for in seven years his time seems to have passed. . . ."

In 1968, Eldridge Cleaver had been all things revolutionary. A parolee from an earlier conviction, he had been acting head of the Black Panther Party which FBI Director J. Edgar Hoover labeled as the "greatest threat" to the nation's security among a host of revolutionary groups; he had been the most eloquent and vitriolic of anti-Establishment spokesmen: author, social critic, reporter for the *Ramparts* magazine. He had been the rabid advocate of tearing down the nation's walls. Caught in a shoot-out with Oakland police in 1968, he had been wounded, jailed, released on

$50,000 bail only to become a presidential candidate for the Peace and Freedom Party. As such he declared the first thing he would do if elected would be to "burn down the mother," meaning the White House. Scheduled to return to jail November 27, 1968, the candidate, who was ineligible to run for the presidency because he was only thirty-three years old, disappeared just hours before he was to report. Only weeks before, he had managed to get some 30,000 votes at the polls.

His return promised to be everything that the "man bites dog" press continually looked for. Not only was he a prominent fugitive returning; the Cleaver now in custody was vastly different from the earlier one. As different as the airport was from his heydays of the sixties. Except for agents and newsmen, Cleaver's return was void of the former clamor. No demonstrators or supporters thronged around to offer help; his Black Panther Party was in other hands now. Life in America was quiet, almost sedate.

So were Cleaver's new words. Gone was his former savage, four-letter vocabulary. Of late he had been reported as saying, as he did in an article written earlier but printed on the *New York Times'* Op-Ed page the day of his return:

"With all of its faults, the American political system is the freest and most democratic in the world."

Considering he had once called the United States "the Number 1 obstacle to human progress," that was a startling admission. He made even more startling comments in the *New York Times'* article:

"Each generation subjects the world it inherits to severe criticism. I think that my generation has been more critical than most, and for good reason. At the same time, at the end of the critical process, we should arrive at some conclusions. We should have discovered which values are worth conserving. It is the beginning of another fight, the fight to defend those values from the blind excesses of our fellows who are still caught up in the critical process. It is my hope to make a positive contribution in this regard."

Old Black Panther friends were to call him a traitor for that. Law officials were to snort. The press would be filled with skepticism for months because even stranger, more incredible changes were to be disclosed in the character of Eldridge Cleaver.

But all that was to come—

All he replied to reporters that day at Kennedy Airport when they asked him why he had come back was, "I think a situation exists in the country now where I can have my day in court."

He would have his day in court. Meanwhile the nation's press, astounded at Cleaver's behavior from November, 1975, to the present, still asks, Where is this guy coming from anyway?

Well, where *is* he coming from?

ACKNOWLEDGMENTS

Grateful acknowledgment is made to the publishers, authors and copyright owners of works quoted in this book for permission to reprint excerpted materials.

Excerpts from *Soul on Ice* by Eldridge Cleaver, copyright © 1968 by Eldridge Cleaver. Used with permission of McGraw-Hill Book Company.

Excerpts from *Conversation with Eldridge Cleaver* by Lee Lockwood, copyright © 1970 by Lee Lockwood and Eldridge Cleaver. Used with permission of McGraw-Hill Book Company.

Exerpts from *The Black Panthers* by Gene Marine, copyright © 1969 by Gene Marine. Reprinted by arrangement with the New American Library, Inc., New York.

Excerpts from news accounts from the *Oakland Tribune*, April 7 and 8, 1968, copyright © 1968 by the *Oakland Tribune*. Reprinted with permission.

Excerpts from articles in the *National Courier*, copyright © 1976 the *National Courier*, Division of Logos International Fellowship, Inc., Plainfield, New Jersey. Reprinted by permission.

News accounts from the *San Francisco Examiner*, April 18, 1971 and June 18, 1976, copyright © 1971 and 1976 by the *San Francisco Examiner*. Used by permission.

Excerpts from articles in the January 20, 1969 and December 6, 1975 issues of *The Nation*. Reprinted with permission.

Excerpts from "Old Panther with a New Purr," *Newsweek*, March 17, 1975, copyright © 1975 by *Newsweek*, Inc. All rights reserved. Reprinted by permission.

Excerpts from news accounts from *The New York Times* September 7, 1969; November 1, 1970; January 16, 1977; copyright 1969 / 1970 / 1977 by The New York Times Company. Reprinted by permission.

Excerpts from *Born Black* by Gordon Parks, copyright © 1970, 1971 by Gordon Parks. Reprinted by permission of J.B. Lippincott Company.

BOOK ONE

THE TIMES—A MEMO

CHAPTER ONE

Every journalist with any opportunity at all to do a story on Eldridge Cleaver in the months since his return has tried to come up with an answer to the big question, tried to find some meaning to Eldridge's reappearance—especially since his reappearance has had a kind of resurrection quality about it.

These days, Eldridge is proclaiming Jesus Christ as his Savior. In this dramatic 180-degree turn from his former, ice-filled raging stance, he is telling audiences, "Since I have met Christ I have not met anyone I don't love. Everybody is my brother or my sister. . . ."

Incredible. It boggles the mind, this language. But there is just as much the clear ring of truth in his current words as there used to be in his raging ones.

So the big question persists: *Where is this guy coming from anyway?*

* * * *

You cannot understand any man apart from his

times, the times that make him and the times he helps make. We're not very far removed from Eldridge's violent sixties, but the times that cover his life span go back to the years of the Great Depression in the 1930s. Actually, they go back much farther, if you want to get philosophical. If a man really wanted to do a full biography on him, he'd follow Alex Haley's pattern for his already famous *Roots*, and go back to some Cleaver counterpart of Kunta Kinte. That kind of geneological detective work takes time though, and the big question about Eldridge begs for some kind of answer now. So let's mark out some biographical time boundaries and set the framework of Eldridge's times as from his birth in 1935 to the present, winter-spring, 1977.

The Great Depression strangled America in the thirties and put the whole nation on an economic torture rack. Oddly enough, black people felt its effects, in some ways, less than the whites. Economic depression was their natural condition, their daily way of life. White Americans choked at the contrast between the affluent twenties and the poverty years that followed. So, many black folks took it like sixty-eight-year-old Clifford Burke told Studs Terkel in *Hard Times* (Random House, Inc., Pantheon Books, 1970, p. 104): "The Negro was born in depression. It didn't mean too much to him, the Great American Depression, as you call it. There was no such thing. The best he could be is a janitor or a porter or a shoeshine boy. It only became official when it hit the white man. If you can tell me the difference between the depression today (late sixties) and the Depression of 1932 for a black man, I'd like to know it. Now it's worse, because of the prices. . . ."

Demonstrations and riots have always been a part of Eldridge's times. All the histories of black people, which filled in so passionately the many gaps left out of the country's education for nearly two hundred years, pointed this out in the most extreme terms. However, even more reasoned accounts, like black historian John Hope Franklin's *From Slavery to Freedom*, tell of turmoil in the year Eldridge was born. Intense feeling against the white landlords in Harlem touched off a wild riot in March, 1935. A black boy, caught stealing a knife from a store was rumored to be beaten to death. Actually, he had escaped, but crowds of blacks gathered and accused police of brutality and the merchants of discrimination. In the rioting that burst out and lasted all night as crowds smashed some two hundred stores and looted shelves, three blacks were killed and over two million dollars worth of damage was done (Franklin, p. 540).

Ghettoes like Harlem had been forming and growing for years. They mushroomed especially during and after World War I. The years leading up to the Depression were jammed with clashes between whites and blacks in the crowding cities over who had priorities for work or membership in unions which repeatedly refused to let in black workers. And when the recession hit in the late twenties, foretelling the Depression to come, blacks were the first to become unemployed. That was what Clifford Burke meant. When the Depression finally did hit, the blacks had already suffered economic hardship for several years.

Among its other evils, the Depression helped spread white racism.

The year 1935 itself was notable in many ways.

5

President Franklin Roosevelt, scurrying around putting emergency measures into effect, set up the Social Security Administration for the elderly, (which excluded agricultural workers, among whom were thousands of blacks), created the Soil Conservation Act to stop massive soil erosion in the nation's breadbasket (remember the Dust Bowl?), and established the Resettlement Administration to help the thousands of farmers who had been forced to abandon their homes because of the dust storms. He put the Works Progress Administration and the Civilian Conservation Corps and other programs into operation to help get people into some kind of employment. It was the year, also, when John L. Lewis of the United Mine Workers formed the CIO to compete with the AF of L and even tried to organize black union membership in the deep South. But too few blacks joined and he failed. Despite everybody's efforts millions were still out of work, hundreds of thousands hungry, scrounging for food anywhere. Some snatched rotting bananas from wharves in New Orleans.

1935 saw other violence than just among the frustrated unemployed. U.S. Senator from Louisiana Huey Long, a veritable dictator in the state, was assassinated. Overaseas, another dictator, Benito Mussolini, sent his troops into a tiny country called Ethiopia.

Some things took people's minds off all these distresses. The blacks gained a new hero when Joe Louis knocked out the six-foot-six, 300-pound Primo Carnera en route to becoming the world's heavyweight boxing champ. George Gershwin's play, *Porgy and Bess*, opened on Broadway. *Amos n' Andy*, a radio program that three decades later would have caused another riot, made blacks and whites alike laugh.

Those were just some of the beginnings of Eldridge Cleaver's times, in that year, 1935.

One night after watching an episode of the TV version of Alex Haley's *Roots*, I lay in bed thinking of what he had gone through to get the sense of his ancestor Kunta Kinte's feelings in the hold of a slave trader. Haley had taken an ocean voyage and laid on a plank night after night to learn how it felt.

I had also been rereading John Howard Griffin's *Black Like Me*. A white Texan, he learned what it meant to be black by dyeing his skin and crossing the color barrier—in the reverse of so many blacks who have tried to become white—and lived for a while as a black in the Deep South.

In the preface to his book Griffin wrote in 1959: "This may not be all of it. It may not cover all the questions, but it is what it is like to be a Negro in a land where we keep the Negro down. . . . I offer it in all its crudity and rawness. It traces the changes that occur to heart and body and intelligence when a so-called first-class citizen is cast on the junkheap of second-class citizenship."

How could I show Eldridge Cleaver's times without doing something as Griffin or Haley had? I had lived most of my life so far removed from the black world that I had paid too little attention to its problems.

More Americans were so far removed from the black world that they simply disregarded it, under-emphasized it, misunderstood it. At times they were so far from the black world, that, in their white one, blacks didn't even exist. At best, they were an unimportant part of the white world's life. And thus, unimportant and largely disregarded, the blacks were forgotten. What injustices and trials which that black world suffered were acknowledged but regarded as being really far less important than the problems the white world had of its own. What directly affects one, in other words, is most important and dealt with first, or worse, even to the exclusion of all the lesser, more distant, matters.

But if whites were separated from blacks, and even from the bitterer horrors of the Depression, we still joined the rest of the nation in thrilling to Joe Louis. I yelled when he clobbered Primo Carnera, beat Jim Braddock to become world heavyweight champ, and flattened Max Schmeling in their return match in 1938. (That was a victory over the Nazis as much as a black man's triumph over a white man.) Joe Louis was just as much a hero to me as he was to so many blacks. And I felt the same when Jesse Owens triumphed in the 1936 Olympics.

Among the scores of different kinds of worlds in this country, one was black and one was white, and within the white one was another sub-white-world of people to whom blacks were blacks in name only.

We helped make up the times Eldridge walked through as he grew up, times that saw the first issue of *Life* magazine in 1936, read *Gone with the Wind* in 1937, and followed Horatio Hornblower in the *Saturday Evening Post* for years. And, of course, whether you were around or not you'll remember Norman Rockwell's *Post* covers; everybody, black and white, loved Rockwell.

Everybody loved the movie version of *Gone with the Wind* in 1939, too. Some three hundred thousand persons lined the streets in Atlanta for seven miles to watch Clark Gable and Vivien Leigh ride by to the premiere showing, and millions more jammed theaters from coast to coast. But 1939 closed out the decade on sharply divergent notes—increasing optimism at the end of the Depression and increasing fear over the growth of Nazi power. Already England and France were in the war. It was only a matter of time before America joined too.

What lots of folks don't realize is that 1939 was really a remarkable year. In retrospect it stands out, among other things, for the refusal of the Daughters of the American Revolution to let singer Marian Anderson perform in Constitution Hall in Washington—and for Secretary of the Interior Harold L. Ickes' prompt invitation for Miss Anderson to give her recital on the steps of the Lincoln Memorial. She did, and on Easter Sunday, seventy-five thousand people attended.

But most Americans' minds in 1939 were on the nation's two fantastic world's fairs in San Francisco and New York (the latter drew 33 million visitors). People listened to the black bands of Duke Ellington and Count Basie. Women were especially happy. The strange new fabric, nylon, which would make much finer hosiery than silk was now commercially available. Hardly anybody comprehended what was in store when the first television program was beamed from the Empire State Building that year, but millions deplored the shocking behavior of America's greatest air hero, Charles A. Lindbergh. He had accepted a medal from Nazi Field Marshal Hermann Goering and had come home extolling German technology and industriousness and preaching isolationism.

9

However, in September, 1939, when Hitler invaded Poland, everybody listened apprehensively. What they had feared throughout the decade was here at last: Europe was at war, and the United States was sure to get in it, too. People glued their ears even more tightly to their radios to hear the latest from Walter Winchell and H.V. Kaltenborn, and to find out what Franklin Delano Roosevelt would say in the latest of his continuing "fireside chats."

The year ended internationally as it had begun, on the harsh note of war. In the previous February, General Francisco Franco had emerged victorious in the Spanish Civil War; by December France and England were at war with Germany and Finland still resisted Russian armies.

One other thing was also part of 1939 times: Dr. Albert Einstein had written President Roosevelt that year that nuclear fission was a possibility. The atom bomb was in the world's womb.

CHAPTER TWO

The new decade was to put man and God in closer relationship. Already in the latter part of the thirties, stories were coming out of Europe about the godlessness of Hitler's regime—indeed the atrocities made it all too plain that man's only hope was in God. Americans, always insisting they were Christian, were really more deistic than Christian, declaring a God-man faith more than a Christ-man faith. But the Depression saw countless prayers rise heavenward for relief from the sorrows brought on by unemployment and hunger.

Largely a liberal theology was preached from the nation's pulpits. Modernism and Bible-believing fundamentalism were crossing swords. The best-known preachers, like Harry Emerson Fosdick, mixed so much of the new Freudian psychology in with their Bible verses that their doctrine often appeared more Freudian than Christian.

Nominal Christianity was prevalent. Liberalism and psychology—these constituted America's religions increasingly through the thirties.

And although this was to continue, the focus shifted sharply in the forties. Bishop Fulton J. Sheen's Catholic Hour was on ninety-five radio stations in 1940 and he was getting three to six thousand letters a day. In Germany, *Time* magazine told Americans, Pastor Martin Niemoller cried, "Not you, Herr Hitler, but God is my Fuehrer," and millions of Germans echoed his defiance. Hitler raged back, "It is Niemoller or I," and imprisoned the pastor. GIs released him in 1945.

The Salvation Army's bell-ringing legions were always on street corners at Christmastime, but most Americans looked at *religious* people as somewhat odd, the way they eyed Jehovah's Witnesses in 1940 when police from Maine to Texas rounded the sectarians up as alleged spies and fifth columnists because they refused to salute the flag or declare allegiance to the government. Of the Bible-believing Christians in America as the forties arrived, just a remnant believed the "old time" way.

But when war hit in 1941 matters changed abruptly. Faith in God had to save them then. God went to war along with their fathers, sons and daughters. GIs wrote home about being saved when a bullet hit their pocket New Testament, and told about God directing military movements and saving embattled platoons. "Foxhole" religion was often joked about, but it was real to too many GIs in the foxholes to be mocked. And so, on the lips of American leaders and soldiers and anxious families alike, God, if not Christ, became a more familiar part of the decade.

What else needs to be recalled of the forties? Certainly not the course of the war; that is still being replayed on late night television, battle by battle. 1940 brought the draft; 1941, Pearl Harbor; the years that followed, heroic courage, family heartache, ration stamps, Ernie Pyle's poignant frontline dispatches and Bill Mauldin's Willy and Joe. But what about the problem of America's blacks? Oh, yes, that problem was part of the war, too, first with the excessively high percentage of draft registration rejections (three times that of whites, because of educational deficiencies and social diseases), then with discrimination in the armed services. These were alleviated somewhat in time, but they were reminders that the problem still festered. The more observable portion was at home, though. Blacks encountered widespread refusals of employment when they sought work at defense plants. The government made some verbal gestures towards overcoming this discrimination, but words achieved nothing. In 1941, A. Philip Randolph, president of the Brotherhood of Sleeping Car Porters and one of the original vice presidents of the CIO after John L. Lewis had organized it in 1935, advanced the idea of a massive march on Washington of perhaps even one hundred thousand persons to insure blacks of fair employment treatment. Blacks responded eagerly and plans were made for a march on July 1.

Embarrassed Washington officials asked themselves what Berlin would think of this, a nation claiming equality for all suddenly exposed for its racial discrimination. By June, when thousands were preparing to entrain for Washington, President Roosevelt sought out Randolph to try to head off the humiliation. Randolph stuck to his guns and got the president to issue Executive Order 8802 against discrimination of any kind in defense industries because of race, creed, color or national origin. The order became a part of every defense contract. It was hailed as the greatest step forward since Lincoln's Emancipation Proclamation.

But laws don't change people's hearts. Blacks, along with other ethnic minorities, were invading northern industrial communities in growing numbers, increasing communal social pressures. The worst race riot of the war broke out in Detroit on June 20, 1943, when a white man and a black man got into a fist fight that set whites and blacks fighting throughout most of the city. President Roosevelt had to send six thousand soldiers in to patrol the streets. After more than thirty hours of rioting, twenty-five blacks and nine whites lay dead and several hundred thousand dollars worth of property had been destroyed.

That made big enough headlines for everyone to notice, but another event in 1943 went unheralded, except by blacks (and how many of them even noticed at the time?) and a smattering of whites: George Washington Carver died. Once a slave, he had made a name for himself as an agricultural chemist. He was a renowned professor at Alabama's Tuskegee Institute and had joined Booker T. Washington there and for forty-five years had advised Southern farmers how to improve their lands. He created more than three hundred synthetic materials from the lowly peanut, including paint, soap, ink, dyes and even nitroglycerine. He hadn't been free from discrimination; his achievements came in spite of the surrounding prejudices. He was the black man's Thomas Edison, but the American public paid little attention to Dr. Carver's passing.

The forties, however, were to see the two separate worlds of whites and blacks coming inexorably closer together. In the Depression years the two worlds had been far enough apart for most white Americans to remain personally unconcerned about the blacks. The war thrust blacks and whites together in combat, industry and neighborhood, sometimes amicably but more often violently.

Five hundred black GIs landed at Omaha Beach on D-Day while black antiaircraft units helped protect the Normandy beachhead and defend Allied gains in North Africa and Italy. Black engineers built the Ledo Road in Burma, the Stilwell Road in China, and tied Canada and Alaska together via the Alcan Highway. Lieutenant General Benjamin O. Davis, Sr. became the war's highest-ranked black officer; and his son was later to become an Air Force general. The armed services had opportunity for more camaraderie than existed before between blacks and whites, but discrimination was still alive.

At home, thronging to the higher paying defense jobs, blacks and whites alike came from rural areas to the big cities where lack of housing dumped them and the cities' residents onto each other's laps. In Los Angeles County, in the period from 1940-45 alone, the black population jumped from 75,000 to 150,000. Heaped atop the large Mexican population, interracial clashes increased. The Cleavers moved into this atmosphere at the close of the war. Millions of GIs came home to readjust to civilian life. Personal problems once more allowed little time for race matters.

Once the nation had gotten over President Roosevelt's death in April, 1945, it moved from shock to doomsday fear over the atom bomb at Hiroshima and Nagasaki. Then it had settled down after the relief and joy of V-E and V-J Days, but the tempo and tension of the black-white worlds on collision course seemed to double. The NAACP and other organizations pressed for full equality; the nation's consciousness considered the glorious principles of the United Nations and began to frown at the problems of the racially mixed cities.

The presidency underwent a readjustment, too. FDR's successor was like him only by being also a Democrat. However, President Truman made some significant improvements in the climate to favor the betterment of blacks. In 1946, he appointed several commissions which issued reports denouncing the denial of civil rights and demanding an early end to segregation, an echo, but firmer in resolve, of FDR's 1941 executive order that staved off Randolph's threatened march on Washington. It was a valiant try, but the ghettoes in major cities continued to overflow as the community unrest which would one day be labeled "urban crisis" simmered and sizzled, heading for the middle fifties, by which time Truman's anti-discrimination doctrine would be considered empty words.

Yet, characteristic of the contradictions of the last half of the decade were the breaking of the color barrier in baseball when Jackie Robinson signed with the Brooklyn Dodgers in 1947, and the emergence of Dr. Ralph Bunche as a man of significance at the United Nations. That same year saw Martin Luther King, Jr. ordained as a minister in his father's church in Atlanta. And about this time Eldridge Cleaver was having his first run-in with authorities in Los Angeles for bike-stealing.

Despite all this, America's black-white problem remained in the background, held down, if not totally suppressed, by other national stresses like shifts in the economy due to industrial labor strife and the continuing personal individual readjustment unavoidable in such times.

Food rationing on all items but sugar ended in November, 1945; a year later all wage and price controls were lifted except from rents, rice and sugar; sugar rationing hung on until June, 1947. In 1946, the government had to seize the railroads to stave off an impending strike, but workers struck anyway six days later. And United Mine Worker President John L. Lewis was constantly at odds with President Truman. Twice the beetle-browed Lewis and the government wrestled to the mat in 1946, once in May with Truman seizing the soft coal mines and again in November when Lewis defied a government injunction and called miners out of the pits. In 1947, Lewis threatened again and won his demands without a strike; yet by year's end he was causing more trouble, this time telling the American Federation of Labor that the United Mine Workers was disaffiliating itself from that union. Nationwide strikes continued in 1948.

God had come home from the war, too. GIs who had praised the Lord while they passed ammunition brought their foxhole religion home to local churches.

Americans listened avidly to the resonantly reassuring and compassionate voice of the man portraying Jesus Christ on Goodyear's radio series, *The Greatest Story Ever Told*. While many were paying attention to Dale Carnegie, others listened to their local pastors, read books by Norman Vincent Peale and Fulton Oursler or heeded Monsignor Fulton J. Sheen's admonitions. Hitler's example of man's inhumanity to man required much reaffirmation of Christian faith. Readjustment to a new, faster, more technological, racial world hit jabbingly at man's spirit. "The brotherhood of man" arose as a new catch phrase.

Despite all that, not too many white Americans—or black either, for that matter—outside of South Carolina paid any attention at all to a district court's ruling that blacks could not be excluded from voting in the state's Democratic primary in 1947, or that 35,000 did vote there in the 1948 primary, or that by 1948 the number of registered black voters in Georgia already numbered more than 150,000. Politics and voter equality held people's attention only sporadically anyway, and nobody was interested in such matters if they were in some state a thousand miles or more away from them.

* * * *

All of these movements continued as the fifties arrived with a flush of national fervor opening the second half of the twentieth century. The table of contents in *Time's Capsule* history of 1950 lists as the "Events of the Year" Dr. Bunche's winning of the Nobel Peace Prize, television's nationwide popularity (the number of sets jumped from three million to ten million that year), George Bernard Shaw's death, the Korean War, and the failure of Puerto Rican assassins to take the life of President Truman.

Time's list also noted a new aspect of postwar

18

America: war on Communist spies. Alger Hiss was found guilty of perjury; his prosecutor was a man named Richard Nixon. Ethel and Julius Rosenberg were arrested and Senator Joseph McCarthy of Wisconsin began his drive against alleged Communist subversives in the United States.

However, the opening note of the decade was patriotism. There was much praiseful but analytic reevaluation of the "USA—The Permanent Revolution," as *Fortune* magazine called it. Many stopped to reflect on the state of the nation, but such meditation didn't stop the march of events.

People reflected on Joe Louis in his prime and were sad to hear him announce, after being outjabbed by Ezzard Charles in their 1950 rematch, "I'll never fight again." An American hero passed from the stage; however, the blacks still had theirs in Charles. Baseball fans reflected sadly, too, when the great Connie Mack finally stepped down from his Philadelphia Athletics' post.

Milton Berle, Ed Sullivan, and Kukla, Fran and Ollie vied for attention on some eight million television sets in 45 million homes while an embryonic Women's Liberation attitude got support from Lynn White, Jr., president of all-girl Mills College in Oakland, California. He declared many women in 1950 were still clinging to the "biologically fantastic notion that to be different from men is to be inferior to men."

Fears of Communist subversion floated in the air, thanks to the Berlin Airlift a few years earlier, the Cold War and Senator McCarthy's increasingly ominous accusations of spies everywhere in American government. The University of California regents and faculty fought over whether teachers should sign a loyalty oath as to their past or present membership in the Communist party. A bestseller of 1950 was *The God That Failed* by twenty ex-Party members. Notable people like authors Arthur Koestler, Andre Gide and Richard Wright, told what they had seen and why they had bolted from Communist ranks.

* * * *

The most succinct but also most elaborate attempt to wrap up the "American Way of Life" for those Americans who did want to reflect at the century's half-way mark came in *Fortune* magazine's special edition of February, 1951. It called the ever-changing but never-changing character of America *The Permanent Revolution*.

The national foundations, of course, as laid down by the Declaration of Independence were the unalienable rights granted by our Creator: life, liberty and the pursuit of happiness. The cornerstone of these is the right to life. To guarantee this right—to *stay* alive—man must be free. He must have the liberty to seek ways to feed, clothe and shelter himself. Such right to liberty implies also freedom of choice, the right to be happy in his pursuit of food, clothing and shelter. The basic right was life. The goal was a life of happiness. Liberty thus becomes the basic requirement to guarantee the first right and assure the ultimate goal. That basic proposition was America's golden nugget, its pearl of great price.

That proposition allowed for diversity, said *Fortune's* editors, and permitted ultimate flexibility. It thus both recognized and accounted for the constant change in America. Also it made not for the "American Way of Life," but for American "ways" of life.

Inherent also in the life-liberty-pursuit of happiness proposition was the right to own property. If one man was happier owning property—home, business or other material possessions, fine. If not, if he wanted to be an employee instead of an employer, that was also fine. The proposition allowed that flexibility; thus came the upward or downward economic mobility that changing times or changing choices incurred. The Permanent Revolution then is really the permanent changeableness.

Since the Declaration of Independence had noted that "all men are endowed by their Creator with certain unalienable Rights," then all men, equally, shared in the flexibility, mobility and changeableness. The basic proposition thus applied to the individual, providing the guarantees whereby he could develop to his fullest potential, physically and spiritually.

Assessing all this in their mid-century review, *Fortune's* editors noted the problems of free men, pointing out that the permanent problem in the Permanent Revolution is the continuing conflict over goals: With life, food, clothing and shelter being physically perceived, the goals become physical or material. And these conflict with the goals arising from man's second perception of himself as a spiritual creature. Thus he has spiritual needs, as well as physical ones, which aim him in the direction of those goals. Material and spiritual goals often oppose one another, so the permanent problem is how to reconcile this conflict.

21

"This central focus of the American way of life—the human individual," wrote *Fortune*, "was born politically in the Age of Reason . . . but spiritually it goes back to the founding of Christianity, whence the American derives his basic concept of the individual. . . .

"The idea of the perfectibility of man, for example, which gives Americans so much drive, is a Christian ideal. And the democratic virtues which have to do with the relation of one man to another, are essentially Christian virtues. . . ."

What *Fortune* didn't say was that, along with the political birth in the Age of Reason of the idea of the individual, the Age of Reason also produced the concept of man's faith in himself—humanism, which altered the real focus of Christianity, faith in God in Christ, to faith in man as a creature able to perfect himself.

Not saying this led the magazine's editors to miss the precise target when they added very perceptively "The American's Christianity is, to be sure, somewhat one-sided; his idea of 'perfectibility,' for example, is theologically naive: his optimism leads him to overlook some of the profounder, more tragic depths of the human soul; he is apt to translate spiritual truths too facilely into practical terms. . . ."

Absolutely true as far as it goes. The idea of perfectibility—the optimistic view of man, born out of the optimistic Age of Reason assumes man can perfect himself. But the Bible says only God in Christ can perfect man. This conflict between humanism and the God of the Bible had been going on for centuries at America's point at the mid-twentieth-century mark, and it would continue with increasing fervor in the next two decades.

The American is a busy, busy citizen in operating the unique American system through some 200,000 clubs, committees, councils, leagues, lodges, political parties and societies "to cope with everything from World War III, wrecked homes and smog, to such causes as that forwarded by the National Society to Discourage the Use of the Name Smith for Purposes of Hypothetical Illustration."

Included in that list, of course, are all the civil liberties and rights with which the next two decades at least would be so violently involved. *Fortune* did comment on the nation's race problem, though: "Few would debate the assertion that the greatest failure of American democracy has been its failure to achieve a real emancipation of the Negro. . . ."

It's interesting to note that in perhaps eighty pages or so of text on America's Permanent Revolution, *Fortune* devoted barely more than half a page to that "greatest failure." It is also indicative of just how much attention Americans as a whole were giving to it in 1950.

Beginning just four years down the road they would be giving far more attention to the black problem. Eldridge in 1950 was fifteen, just moving into manhood, already street-seasoned, seeing the basic proposition, the Permanent Revolution, and the "busy, busy" American white people from his world. I was thirty, far removed from the racist part of my white world but becoming more aware of that part. Gaining momentum downhill to the mid-century intersection of 1954, our two worlds were veering more sharply

23

together on their collision course.

* * * *

Between 1950 and then, though, people would read of Ingrid Bergman bearing a son to film director Roberto Rossellini only a week after filing for a Mexican divorce from her previous husband. They gasped in shame at that and in surprise and disbelief at the news that sultry actress Jane Russell, once a scandal for her "uncensored" bed scenes in the notorious movie "Outlaw," had become a "born-again believer in the Lord Jesus Christ."

"Born again?" That smacked of Sunday school and store-front gospel missions and street-corner evangelists. Primitive stuff for sophisticated Americans.

But people also read of a forty-two-hour-and-forty-minute marathon of Christian testimonies by hundreds of students during Evangelistic Week at Wheaton College in Illinois in February, 1950, that filled up the auditorium "and overflowed into a small chapel downstairs" so that "classes had to be canceled altogether." And they would become more and more familiar with a new, powerful Bible-toting evangelist named Billy Graham.

During that period I would move into a smaller part of my white world, farther removed than ever from aggressive Southern white racists but in a domain where many were more subtly racist, by default, from not taking part in the race problem: I became in 1952 a born-again believer in the Lord Jesus Christ. If I sound critical of such Christians regarding the race problem I am thus in the sense of a favorite saying of Eldridge's, "If you're not part of the solution, then you're part of the problem." By shoving our attention of the growing race problem to some "half page" of our lives, as *Fortune* had in its assessment of America, we were definitely not part of even any attempt at a solution. We were part of Eldridge's problem.

Of course, many blacks in Eldridge's world were also part of the problem. When two worlds collided in that intersection in 1954 following the United States Supreme Court's school desegregation decision, a lot of blacks were just as Eldridge wrote in *Soul on Ice:* ". . . I do not believe that I had even the vaguest idea of [the court decision's] importance or historical significance." But they would, and so would my white world, soon have to admit, with Eldridge, ". . . . later, the acrimonious controversy ignited by the end of the separate-but-equal doctrine was to have a profound effect on me."

No matter in 1954 that blacks like Dr. Ralph Bunche received the Nobel Peace Prize, or that Harvard had, back in 1949, hired its first black professor, or that a black man was the Assistant Secretary of Labor in Washington. Those were mere tokens, pebbles on the sharp-edged rocky beach of an endless shore of racial inequalities. Discrimination still existed in jobs and—obviously, according to the Supreme Court—in education. Jim-Crow laws still existed on buses, segregation in hotels and even toilet facilities, and in the teeming ghettoes, poor housing conditions were the rule, not the exception.

So the worlds collided. It was more than a fender-bender.

* * * *

The United States Supreme Court's decision on May 17, 1954, seems to be the prime mover in all that subsequently happened. It did away with the separate-but-equal doctrine and outlawed school segregation. Many racial matters were coming to a head in 1954, but of them all, the court's ruling was the most significant.

Most people didn't appreciate its significance though. Not until its attempted implementation did people pay attention. Virginia's Senator Harry F. Byrd called for massive resistance to it and managed to line up staunch support from all eleven states of the Old Confederacy. Opposition to desegregation stiffened so quickly that everybody's head swam.

In 1955, the NAACP, which had been pushing hard for expansion of civil rights, encountered increasingly violent resistance. Several Southern states declared the organization subversive or saw injunctions issued against any of its further activities. An Arkansas congressman entered forty pages of evidence into the *Congressional Record* that NAACP leaders were un-American.

White citizens' councils arose. In some parts of the South violence was rampant, increasing greatly after George Lee, NAACP leader in Belzoni, Mississippi, was killed with a shotgun blast in the back.

On the blacks' side the opening of the organized civil rights movement began for all intents and purposes in December, 1955, with the Montgomery bus boycott. The Rev. Martin Luther King, Jr. described it in his

26

book, *Stride Toward Freedom*.

Blacks had long been subject to numerous indignities on Montgomery's buses. There were no black drivers, and white drivers were "abusive and vituperative . . ." not uncommonly referring to blacks as "black cows" and "black apes." Frequently, drivers ordered blacks to get off the bus after they had paid their fare and made them enter through the back door. Often buses would pull away with the black's dime before he or she even reached the back door.

The city's buses still had "whites only" sections. Even if a bus was packed and no whites were sitting in the first four seats, blacks couldn't sit there; worse, if whites overflowed their section, blacks had to stand up for them.

This is what led to the arrest of Mrs. Rosa Parks. Tired after work, she boarded a bus, and sat down in the black section. When the bus got overcrowded with whites and the driver asked her to stand and move back, she refused.

As a result of her arrest, blacks met and decided to boycott the buses. They distributed some seven thousand leaflets, saying, "Don't ride the bus to work, to town, to school, or any place Monday, December 5. . . . If you work, take a cab, or share a ride, or walk."

One lady who received a leaflet couldn't read and gave it to her employer who then took it to a local newspaper. The paper ran a front-page story on the plans, thus letting thousands of other blacks know what to do the following Monday.

The boycott leaders had hoped for maybe sixty-five per cent compliance; they got almost one hundred per cent. Montgomery's buses ran empty or near-empty all day long. So the boycott was extended. It was so successful it was tried in Tallahassee and the civil rights movement was born.

Once the ball started to roll it rolled all over. Not only the NAACP or the high court decision, or King's Southern Christian Leadership Conference (really formed somewhat later), but also new white groups gave support, and old black organizations became more active. The increased activity led to increased resistance—and increased violence.

In 1956 students and townsfolk of Tuscaloosa violently opposed the presence of Autherine Lucy, the first black student at the University of Alabama. The regents expelled her when rioting in protest became so rampant. Singer Nat "King" Cole was attacked by whites for singing at the Birmingham city auditorium before an all-white audience.

Throughout the South, states and local school boards repeatedly tried to delay school integration, but with the passage of the Civil Rights Bill of 1957, the Department of Justice gained a Civil Rights Division, providing new federal muscle to force compliance. And when Arkansas Governor Orval Faubus defied a court order to integrate the state's schools that year, claiming Little Rock's schools were now privately owned, President Eisenhower showed the nation that Washington meant business. He sent one thousand paratroopers of the Arkansas National Guard to assure students safe passage to school.

The next day nine black students enrolled in the city's white schools. It was a victory for the civil rights movement. Still, elsewhere, local school boards continued open defiance.

Although the country was uptight and strung out over rights, integration and racist resistance for the rest of the decade, there were other things indicating the shape of things to come in the sixties.

By 1957, the beat generation was already past the toddler stage, as Jack Kerouac's novel, *On the Road*, had been testifying. In 1957, Michigan's State Supreme Court struck down a state law seeking to censor pornographic material, an augury of the many obscenity trials ahead. Later, Vice President Richard Nixon told off Soviet Premier Nikita Krushchev in Moscow and received hurrahs at home for his firm stand, indicative that anticommunism was still in the air and by 1960, people were once again in the throes of a presidential election year.

CHAPTER THREE

As the 1960s began, the Students for a Democratic Society (SDS) had already been formed out of the Student League for Industrial Democracy and radicalized to become one of the bastions of the New Left. Advocating the overthrow of the United States "system," the SDS would move through the next ten civil rights years to where in 1969 an SDSer would emphasize, "It's not reform we're after."

Also in 1960, Dr. Martin Luther King, Jr. organized the Student Non-Violating Coordinating Committee (SNCC) as an integrated civil rights group, attracting many sincerely concerned young blacks and whites to the cause. But by 1961, revolutionaries were already radicalizing it, moving away from Dr. King's pacifist principles (modeled after those of Mahatma Gandhi) toward that of Black Power, Malcolm X militancy. Under Stokely Carmichael, SNCC allied with the Black Panther Party; under H. Rap Brown, Carmichael's successor, it supported international "black" revolution. By 1969, SNCC leader James Forman delivered the "Black Manifesto" demanding $500 million from white churches for past "exploitation" of blacks. Dr. King and the Southern Christian Leadership Conference, however, remained more on the nonviolent end of the civil rights spectrum. Certainly they replied to violent white resistance with increasing strenuous and often violent reactions, but, in the political sense, they were at the opposite pole from SDS and SNCC and other black revolution advocates.

In the swirling social currents of civil rights supporters, self-admitted Marxist activists, antiwar demonstrators and young people down on the Establishment for scores of reasons, new polarizations seemed to appear daily only to combine and recombine again; alliances were made and broken quickly; loyalties shifted not only among participants but among the millions who watched the decade roar at them from their TV sets. Peace and violence walked side by side; whites and blacks opposed each other and fought bitterly; and law-and-order backlash suffered the same fate.

* * * *

The decade opened quietly enough on the East Coast. On February 1, 1960, four black students from the Agricultural and Technical College in Greensboro, North Carolina, walked into a variety store, bought a few things and sat down at a lunch counter for some coffee. Because they were black they were refused service. So they simply sat and waited until the store closed.

31

Their patience marked a new twist in the nonviolent civil rights movement.

Three thousand miles away on the West Coast a different kind of protest broke out. In May, when the House Un-American Activities Committee returned to San Francisco to resume its investigations of allegedly subversive teachers, it ran into much greater disfavor than it had on its first run in 1959. Hostile witnesses demonstrated inside the hearing room while students picketed outside. In the three-day fracas, police dragged demonstrators downstairs, roughed them up, and turned high-pressure hoses on the crowds. After the third day, which found five-thousand demonstrators on hand, J. Edgar Hoover declared the acts were Communist-inspired.

The news media also became participants, helping to make all the events of nationwide interest and concern. Americans were *there*, everywhere, vicariously participating via TV screens. With the smallest of events often given overweighted prominence, every event captured national attention.

So when Freedom Rides in 1961 replaced the 1960 sitting in at white restaurants, wading-in at white beaches and sleeping-in in white hotel lobbies, all America saw Freedom Riders attacked in Anniston, Alabama. They also learned of victory the moment it happened, when the Interstate Commerce Commission banned segregation on all interstate buses and trains and in all terminals.

In 1962, the nation watched James Meredith, protected by federal marshals, enroll at the University of Mississippi—and took a breather when John Glenn became the first American to orbit the earth, thereby distracting folks from the earth's turmoil.

We all watched 1963 unfold its horrors: Birmingham officials unleashing squads of police with dogs, cattle prods and fire hoses against Dr. King's demonstrators who threw rocks and bottles back in return, resulting in thousands of schoolchildren being arrested, and stores and apartment houses destroyed, by some twenty-five hundred rioters; Medgar Evers' murder; the march on Washington where the 200,000 who came peacefully heard Dr. King declare, "I have a dream . . . "

We all watched Dallas in horror November 22, as one assassin killed President Kennedy, saw the burden of the presidency shift onto Lyndon Johnson's shoulders, then pressed white knuckles to our lips as a second assassin murdered the first before our very eyes.

By February, 1965, when Malcolm X was assassinated we had become almost addicted to civil violence. Still, on that "Black Sunday" of March 21, we blanched when we saw Dr. King's marchers, many of them clergymen and Catholic nuns, stride through Selma to the Edmund Pettus Bridge to be attacked by state troopers with clubs and tear gas. Appalled when a Unitarian minister from Boston was bludgeoned to death, we watched for five days.

And for another five days in August we saw the Watts area of Los Angeles dismembered: more than thirty-five dead, four-thousand arrested, and $40 million worth of property damage inflicted.

There was one thing we didn't see nationwide that year. In Alabama, John Hulett and Stokely Carmichael, tired as were so many workers with the continued white resistance to registering blacks to vote, organized the Lowndes County Freedom

Organization. Blacks were fed up, Hulett said, so "when they go down to vote and they see the white man's guns, they're going to go back home and get theirs. . . . There's going to be some shooting, some bloodshed. . . .

The symbol of their new organization: a black panther. Only after two men in Oakland, Huey Newton and Bobby Seale, pressed their clenched fists together in unity in 1966 to become the first two members of the Oakland Black Panther Party, would the nation take note.

We had to witness the aftermath of the shooting of James Meredith while he was on his pilgrimage from Memphis to Jackson in 1966 first before paying attention to the Black Panthers. The party made headlines in 1967 by using the sophistication many protesters had developed by then: be overly brash and you'll make your point—remember, you're on TV.

So there they came in May, 1967, about twenty Black Panthers, armed with rifles and sidearms, menacing in their black leather jackets and black pants. They strode purposefully into the legislature at the state capital in Sacramento, California, with hordes of newsmen in tow. One later account says it was newsmen who actually led the Panthers into the legislative chamber: it told of TV cameramen and photographers backing down the corridors until some newsmen stumbled backwards into the chamber, thus inadvertently holding the door open as Panthers streamed through to face the stunned politicians.

Few paid any attention to a man named Eldridge Cleaver during that time in Sacramento. Only readers of *Ramparts* would read the raging eloquence of the magazine's new reporter, paroled from prison in late 1966.

Starting in April with riots in Cleveland's black ghetto, turmoil broke out in 159 places across the country. A week-long episode in Detroit saw forty die, two-thousand injured and five-thousand people made homeless as forty-seven hundred paratroopers and eight-thousand National Guardsmen tried to bring the city under control. And in October, upwards of thirty-five thousand antiwar protesters marched on the Pentagon.

The next year would be even worse.

CHAPTER FOUR

1968. Whatever had been coming down for the whole decade came down harder this year.

Individual incidents here are impossible to highlight, let alone detail, save for the biggest of the big headlines. These begin, of course, with the tragic assassinations of Dr. Martin Luther King, Jr. in Memphis, April 4, and of Senator Robert F. Kennedy in Los Angeles, June 5.

Overall statistics for the riot scoreboard tabulate the staggering turbulence:

"In the first few days after the assassination of [Dr.] King . . . the rioting that swept American cities was almost as widespread and destructive as in all of 1967. Last year, 233 racial upheavals in 168 cities and towns caused 82 deaths, 3,400 injuries and 18,000 arrests. By comparison, in April alone this year (1968), 202 racial disturbances hit 172 cities, resulting in 43 deaths, 3,500 injuries and 27,000 arrests . . . The U.S. had 286 racial disturbances from May through the end of August . . ." (*Time Capsule*, 1968, p. 101). Note, those are just *racial* riots.

The National Student Association counted 221 major demonstrations at 101 colleges, according to *Coming Apart* historian O'Neill. Evidence of how outrage was stalking campuses more frequently showed up in April, 1968, as SDS-inflamed students put Columbia University under siege. And in September, with Chicago's political convention ashes still smoldering, militant blacks burst loose on the San Francisco State campus, creating teacher-student strikes that continued for months.

Even the quadrennial national elections were characterized by rage. The political process, which has an ability to generate a distinct hysteria was outdone by the fury of the counterculture protest in August at the Democratic National Convention in Chicago.

Violence feeds on itself and by August the nation had a bellyful. Things had gone so far in the perverted times that the radical, the militant, the revolutionary had become the norm. Months of advertising (thanks to the ever-alert press) helped make Chicago what extremists on both sides warned it would be. As early as November 16, 1967, Jerry Rubin of the newly formed Yippies (Youth International Party)—the extreme Communist portion of the New Left (so extreme that even disciplined Communists disdained their beaded, bearded, bare-chested wildness) announced to the nation: "See you next August in Chicago at the Democratic National Convention. Bring pot, fake delegates' cards, smoke bombs, costumes, blood to throw and all kinds of interesting props. Also football helmets [to counter helmeted, club-bearing, trained shock troops now commonplace]."

Chicago's Mayor Daley and other establishmentarians

retorted in kind, preparing for the worst.

Everybody saw the worst on their TV screens. It was not racial, but antiwar violence. What happened at Chicago exceeded even the worst of the racial conflict.

1968 had other things going for it, too, of course. After all, it *was* a presidential election year. So people voted and put Richard Nixon in office.

But Chicago lingered in memory, burning the nation's conscience. Things had finally gone too far. Freedom required some limits, even in the permissive America of 1968.

Assessing quite accurately the state of the nation, the *Saturday Evening Post* editorialized on the state of the nation in its November 16, 1968, edition: "We are obsessed with violence." Voicing as it did the thoughts of so many in both the white world and black, that editorial is worth excerpting at some length:

"According to a Louis Harris survey, 8 out of 10 Americans agree that law and order have broken down in this country. Politicians have exploited this fear by dramatically agreeing that our cities are uninhabitable, that racial warfare is rampant, that crime is soaring—and that only they or their party can rescue us from being utterly destroyed. Of course the media have given us the evidence with a multimedia presentation of furious violence breaking right up through the cobblestones before our eyes.

" . . . Before we get hysterical about the strains of violence in our national character, there are a few things we ought to consider. First, we are naive to expect ourselves not to be violent. We are the only carnivorous apes, and we would not be here as man today if we were not violent. . . . We are still the only animal that casually kills his own kind . . . and lately we have become . . . fascinated by this. . . ."

Many *Post* readers heartily disagreed with that definition of man, feeling that the magazine had put its finger inadvertently on the *real* root cause of the behavior of the nation's citizenry: mistaken identity. Man came from Eden, not from apes. Man's violence had no familial relation to the violence of animals; it related to man's disobedience to God.

The *Post* spoke for millions of Americans about the years of internecine hatred as it pointed out, "As far as the Negroes are concerned, we have to face the fact that the reservations [those great geographical reservations in the South, just as territorial as those for Indians] are breaking down.

"They have finally come awake and are fighting their way out of the desperate isolation of the countryside and the prison of the ghetto. This has been a fierce struggle, but most of the violence has been committed against property, and it is really extraordinary that these convulsive efforts could be as peaceful as they are."

An accurate commentary on the times. The *Post* had remarks about law and order, also, which were painfully pertinent to the police brutality in Chicago and elsewhere:

". . . The police who have been given the thankless job of maintaining the status quo have been confounded with the escalating problems. The Establishment has always paid the police to protect the Establishment, allowed them to be the custodians of violence in this good cause, but now it is not so simple. . . ."

And then, another reminder: "We are beginning to realize that police are not the law; that it is their responsibility to protect, not to punish. Police officers are confounded to see elements of the Establishment—students, professors, teachers, doctors, businessmen, clergymen along with hippies and yippies—arrayed with the Negroes against them. . . .

"Of course, it is a misconception that cops are more brutal than they used to be—actually they are much less brutal, and they are generally no more brutal than we want them to be. . . .

"It is also a misconception that most violence is racial. . . . The great bulk of violence across this nation is segregated. Most crimes are definitely not interracial. Two-thirds of murders, aggravated assaults and rapes are performed by relatives, friends and acquaintances of the victims. . . ."

The *Post* ended on the note of tragic irony whose truth cut to the bone: "There has never before been the rage for brotherhood that exists today." World War II had seen the same kind of rage, but in the sixties the rage had run rampant on America's home soil. It had been the Civil War all over again.

How commonplace and acceptable the violent times had become is illustrated by an advertisement in the December 6, 1968, issue of *Time* magazine. Selling music, which is supposed to soothe the savage breast, Time/Life Records offered a record album opening with Beethoven's "Leonore Overture No. 3" under the headline: "Age of Revolution—Introductory Album to the Story of Great Music." And the copy below opened with the words, "To the Bastille!"

And so the most violent of the violent years ran out.

* * * *

New President Nixon could claim no credit, but 1969 eased off somewhat because of his promises and initial moves to wind down the Vietnam conflict and bring American boys home. It took months for that to happen though, and before it did, Nixon kept reopening many raw wounds.

Some wounds stayed open by themselves. One such was the trial of Sirhan Sirhan, accused assassin of Senator Kennedy, which began—once the Rose Bowl was out of the way—on January 7, 1969, the same day on which a jetliner with 146 passengers aboard was hijacked to Cuba (a new brand of terrorism was already underway).

Nostalgic by nature the nation turned wistful on January 10 with the announcement that the 147-year-old *Saturday Evening Post* would cease publication in February. More sadness came in March when former President Eisenhower, then seventy-eight, died.

This mood was blotted out in May, however, by the reminder of the decade's character. In Greensboro, North Carolina, where those four black students in 1960 had sat in so patiently, students from the same college traded shots for three days with National Guardsmen.

Headlines at the same time told about squabbling between students at the University of California at Berkeley and the Board of Regents over a small park near the campus which belonged to the university but which people had dolled up with shrubs, flowers and playground equipment. The regents said no and students insisted yes. The area simmered until May 15, when gas-masked National Guardsmen plus some 250 police and highway partolmen with helicopters and Mace put the entire city under military control. They fenced off the park and rounded up protesters. One onlooker was killed, 100 persons hurt and 1,000 arrested.

Add those incidents to President Nixon's speech at a small Midwestern college critical of protesters, admission by the Justice Department of illegal wiretapping of protesters over the years and another speech by the president announcing that some school districts would be allowed to delay the September, 1969, desegregation deadline—and it's easy to see why 1969 still seemed just a continuation of the year before. Actually there were more campus clashes in 1969, but they were less violent.

But before the year was out it would see the Sharon Tate murders, the Woodstock Rock Festival, a dusk-to-dawn curfew in Hartford, Connecticut after ghetto troubles and firebombing, Harvard teachers voting for the end of the war, 100 persons arrested in Chicago after rioting in the Loop section, and Black Panther leader Bobby Seale bound to his chair and gagged because of his repeated outbursts in the Chicago Seven trial. (It was known as the Chicago Eight trial at first, but the judge finally separated Seale from the others and sentenced him to four years in prison for contempt. This added fuel to revolutionary fires so that defense lawyers and the remaining seven had even more ammunition for denouncing justice as practiced in the

United States.)

Writers of all kinds, sociologists, historians and newsmen, are still analyzing the sixties. One of the best attempts is a previously mentioned book by Rutgers historian William O'Neill, the title of which is especially descriptive: *Coming Apart*. The nation very nearly did just that.

CHAPTER FIVE

The seventies are still so much with us they need little detailing.

Violence has continued, moving into the terrorism of the Third World Liberation Front, the Symbionese Liberation Army, international skyjackings and kidnappings for ransom with threats of death for a host of reasons and causes. The Black Panther Party cried "police harassment" for years and currently has a $100 million lawsuit against the FBI, CIA and IRS for "illegal and systematic efforts to destroy the party since 1967." Although they still cry injustice, much of the Panthers' former vehemence has been channeled into food distribution centers and community betterment.

New controversies, the roots of which go back years and whose shoots were breaking the social and cultural soil long before the violent sixties, have arisen over such things as man-versus-technology, men-versus-Women's Lib and, the most well-publicized, man-versus-Mother Earth in the great environmental debates.

The 1970s were simultaneously christened, dedicated and baptized "The Environmental Decade" on Earth Day, April 22, 1970. Not even the civil rights movement had that kind of introduction.

Earth Day made all the demonstrations of the past puny by comparison. Nearly twenty million people participated. It was the largest, cleanest, most orderly, most peaceful demonstration America had ever witnessed. Environmental Action, a national clearing house for environmental activism, prepared for the great day by coordinating with local groups on 2,000 college campuses in 2,000 communities and in 10,000 high schools throughout the country. When April 22 arrived, throngs met at almost as many places, with noted speakers declaring guilt and goals in all the terms which everyone now considers common language: overpopulation, air pollution, water pollution, urban sprawl, land use and abuse, shabby subdivisions, predatory developers and industrial polluters.

And the seventies have seen Watergate and the dismantling of President Nixon's White House with all the chain reaction that political fissioning caused. The nation is still reacting to Watergate in the open climate the scandal created. Witness the FBI house-cleaning, and confessions still appearing, and the continuing congressional probes of the CIA. The political and racial atmosphere is different in the mid-seventies from the pre-Watergate years.

Currently we are back to politics and race again, both on higher floors than the street-level times of the sixties, with a new president in the White House and Alex Haley's *Roots* on television. President Carter replaced Black Power with "born again" in newspapers, TV newscasts, and even in *Playboy*, so that Christians walk the corridors of power in Washington far more publicly and acceptably than the quieter ones did in their prayer breakfasts and Bible classes of the past. Haley touched a nerve with his book so that the rootlessness which had haunted the nation's blacks for so long is vanishing. A man's heritage, no matter how lowly, is once again becoming the honorable birthright it should be. Despite the observation that some have made about *Roots* reopening still unhealed racial wounds, Haley has contributed to the new, more contrite, more compassionate climate of this decade. Men who love themselves properly are better able to love their neighbors as themselves.

* * * *

All that amounts to a long memo, but those were—and are—Eldridge Cleaver's times. In many ways those years were no different from other hectic periods. But in other ways they were among the most significant in the nation's, and the world's, history. With the years refreshed in memory it's easier to understand why Eldridge walked through his times as he did—and why he made the choices he did.

BOOK TWO

THE (OLD) MAN

CHAPTER ONE

WRITER

If your hands get too cold, they burn.

On ice, refrigerated in society's cold storage of Folsom Prison, Eldridge Cleaver as Convict No. A-29498 burned that way as he spent much of 1965 hunched over his typewriter in the privacy of his cell on the honor block. That was the glory of being on the honor block: you had privacy when you wanted it. Instead of a cell protected only by bars through which somebody could toss a Molotov cocktail at you, as occasionally happened to inmates, honor block cells had solid steel, dungeon-like doors.

At first the clanging door had chilled Eldridge with fear, reminding him of the first time he had ever been thrown into solitary back at San Quentin. Now, though, his cell wasn't just the ultimate separation within the cellblock prison community that itself was separated from civilization beyond; it was privacy. And Eldridge needed privacy as he emerged from the long hot summer of 1965. He was doing a lot of soul-searching, baring himself as he never had before on paper, looking backwards, inwards, and outwards as he put together impressions and thoughts that made up the black rage. These would appear in 1968 in his book, *Soul on Ice*.

He had been writing for months, but on this Labor Day Sunday, September 5, 1965, he was sitting on his bunk, hunkered over the typewriter on the plywood board he balanced on a little stool for his desk, writing a love letter.

He was trying to tell Beverly Axelrod, his lawyer, how he felt about her, about himself and about life.

In all that would happen between then and 1977, what Eldridge wrote to Mrs. Axelrod and what she wrote back in their short correspondence would be overshadowed and forgotten. All that people would remember out of the raging times would be Eldridge's rage. Tragic. Because in this letter and in the others that flurried between him and Beverly Axelrod were revealed the heart of the man and what was real beneath all the rage.

"Dear Beverly," he typed. "For two charged days and restless nights after you left, I loafed in the case of my skull, feeling prematurely embalmed in some magical ethered mist dispensed by the dialectic of our contact. When I left you sitting in that little glass cage, which I must somehow learn to respect because it has a special, eternal meaning now, I did not stop or pause. Including the door to that glass cage, and counting the door of my cell, I passed through twelve assorted gates and doors before collapsing on my narrow bed. . . .

"The doors and gates swung open before me as I advanced upon them, as I charged down on them, as if they were activated by photoelectric cells responding to my approach. I walked swiftly, but I felt myself to be running, stumbling, thrashing and flailing with my arms to clear a passage through dense, tangled vines. I spoke to no one, recognized no one, and I felt that no one could see or recognize me. . . .

"I don't believe I can stand you in such massive doses. It may prove lethal.

"I am almost afraid to return to my manuscripts—which themselves seem to cringe from me—after talking with you. I know I shall remain immobile, transfixed, until I've gotten this letter off to you. . . .

"I really have no sense of myself and I have always suffered under the compliments of others, especially my friends. I panic. . . . It's hypocritical of me, but whenever someone says something nice about me, it sort of knocks me for a loop. . . . The things you said sent me spinning. But don't stop, let me suffer—and overcome.

"I feel impelled to express myself to you extravagantly. . . .

"You have tossed me a lifeline. If you only knew how I'd been drowning, how I'd considered that I'd gone down for the third time long ago, how I kept thrashing around in the water simply because I still felt the impulse to fight back and the tug of a distant shore, how I sat in a rage that night with the polysyllabic burden of your name pounding in my brain—Beverly Axelrod, Beverly Axelrod—and out of what instinct did I decide to write you? It was a gamble, . . . and it was right."

Eldridge had been writing numerous attorneys for two reasons; to seek help for his own particular case and to get the black picture wider publicity. His first letter to Beverly Axelrod in San Francisco was one of those.

She had responded, interested, and had come to visit him.

"Let me say this," he continued that Sunday. "I was 22 when I came to prison [for his conviction in 1958] and of course I have changed tremendously over the years. But I had always had a strong sense of myself and in the last few years I felt I was losing my identity. There was a deadness in my body that eluded me. . . .

"Now I know what it was. And since encountering you, I feel life strength flowing back into that spot. My step, the tread of my stride, which was becoming tentative and uncertain, has begun to recover and take on a new definiteness, a confidence, a boldness which makes me want to kick over a few tables. I may even swagger a little. . . .

"Now turn the record over and play the other side," he wrote, striving to be nakedly honest. "I have tried to mislead you. I am not humble at all. I have no humility and I do not fear you in the least. If I pretend to be shy, if I appear to hesitate, it is only a sham to deceive. By playing the humble part, I sucker my fellow men in and seduce them of their trust. . . .

"I am very well aware of my style. My vanity is as vast as the scope of a dream, my heart is that of a tyrant, my arm is the arm of the Executioner. . . . I had planned to run for President of the United States. My slogan? *PUT A BLACK FINGER ON THE NUCLEAR TRIGGER.* 400 years of docility, of being calm, cool and collected under stress and strain would go to prove that I was the man for the job. . . . I had it made—but then came Watts! All my plans went up in smoke! . . ."

He signed it, "Most Emphatically Yours, Eldridge."

52

Beyond the prison walls, people sang *The Impossible Dream*. Within prison Eldridge was living it. A white divorcee, free in the outside world, established in her profession. And a black convict, behind fences, guards, bars and steel doors, who had graduated from high school via a prison correspondence course. It could have been the most perfectly natural fantasy. Maybe it was. I think it was more. Although he wasn't to be paroled for another year, Eldridge was beginning to liberate his soul by communicating, in love, with a woman who offered all those qualities women offer men, plus what all convicts seek—freedom.

Five days later, on September 10, Beverly wrote her reply:

"Dear Eldridge Cleaver: . . . The need for expression is now upon me, having finished the legal matters, and I'm getting panicky. I'm not strong enough to take the safest course, which would be not to widen the subject matter of our correspondence, and I'm having a terrible time trying to say what I want, knowing it will be read by the censors.

"Your letter, which I keep rereading, shows you're going through the same turmoil I am; but I bear the onus of having allowed it. . . .

"Believe this: I accept you. I know you little and I know you much, but whichever way it goes, I accept you. Your manhood comes through in a thousand ways, rare and wonderful. . . .

"About that other side of the record: Did you really think I didn't know? . . .

". . . . I have a few facets myself. I do not fear you, I know you will not hurt me. Your hatred is large, but not nearly so vast as you sometimes imagine; it can be used, but it can also be soothed and softened.

"What an enormous amount of exploring we have to do! I feel as though I'm on the edge of a new world.

"Memo to me: Be rational. It cannot be resolved. The choices: 1. He believes everything he says, but he cannot know, he has no choice; or 2. It's a beautiful put-on because he doesn't know that you would do exactly what you are doing for him anyway; or 3. It's a game to relieve the monotony, conscious or not. Answer: It doesn't make a damn bit of difference, because I can't find out, he can't find out, and it's too late anyway. The only important thing is to get him out, and that was obvious from the first letter, with all lawyerlike objectivity.

"What an awesome thing it is to feel oneself on the verge of the possibility of really knowing another person. Can it ever happen? I'm not sure. . . ."

And Beverly signed her reply, "Sincerely yours. . . ."

Within another five days, Eldridge would send his reply to hers. On September 15, he began, "Your letters to me are living pieces—chunks!—of you, and are the most important things in my life. . . ."

He had always placed great emphasis, he said, "on people really listening to each other . . . But I was not *really* like this when I was out of prison—although the seeds were there, but there was too much confusion and madness mixed in. I was not too interested in communicating with other people—that is not true. What I mean is, I had a profound desire for communicating with and getting to know other people, but I was incapable of doing so, I didn't know how.

"Do you know what shameless thought just bullied

54

its way into my consciousness? That I deserve you, that I deserve to know you and to communicate with you, that I deserve to have all this happening. What have I done to merit this? I don't believe in the merit system. I Am That I Am. No, I will not hurt you.

"Memo to us: 1. He believes everything he says and knows what he is saying; 2. Put-ons are cruel, and how could I be cruel to you? 3. He does not play games. . . . He has plans and dreams, and he is deadly serious. . . . Taking it like you find it is a burn. . . .

"I seek a lasting relationship, something permanent in a world of change, in which all is transitory, ephemeral, and full of pain. We humans, we are too frail creatures to handle such titanic emotions and deep magnetic yearnings, strivings and impulses.

"The reason two people are reluctant to really strip themselves naked in front of each other is because in doing so they make themselves vulnerable and give enormous power over themselves one to the other. How awful, how deadly, how catastrophically they can hurt each other, wreck and ruin each other forever! How often, indeed, they end by inflicting pain and torment upon each other. Better to maintain shallow, superficial affairs. . . .

"Getting to know someone, entering that new world, is an ultimate, irretrievable leap into the unknown. The prospect is terrifying. The stakes are high. The emotions are overwhelming. In human experience, only the perennial themes can move us to such an extent. Death. Birth. The Grave. Love. Hate.

"I do not believe that a beautiful relationship has to always end in carnage. . . ."

Was Eldridge trying to deaden the echoes of Watts

which had exploded only a few weeks before back in July? Views of the world are often clearest in love letters. He had written about Watts in this busy writing period; now he seemed to be seeking to replace Watts memories with something better.

"Beverly, there is something happening between us that is way out of the ordinary. Ours is one for the books, for the poets to draw new inspiration from, one to silence the cynics, and one to humble us by reminding us of how little we know about human beings, about ourselves. I did not know that I had all these feelings inside me. . . .

"I have a bad habit, when speaking of women while only men are present, of referring to women as bitches. This bitch this and this bitch that, you know. . . ."

And he signed this September 15 letter, "Peace. Don't panic, and don't wake up. Dream on. I am Yours. . . ."

The love affair in these letters is as improbable a one as you could hope to find. More than one reader of them has recongized lyric qualities equal to the classic letters between Elizabeth and Robert Browning, and in many ways the chasm between Eldridge and Beverly was as great between Heloise and Abelard, although fortunately the end of Eldridge's affair wasn't as tragic as Abelard's.

* * * *

From his San Quentin days Eldridge had been corresponding with sympathetic attorneys about his own case, prison injustices and civil rights issues Charles R. Garry, the San Francisco Bay Area attorney who became well-known later as the defense counsel for the Black Panthers, recalls receiving letters from Eldridge as early as 1960. He had paid little attention, describing Eldridge's letters as being "typically narrow" in their sectarian religious flavor and view of prison problems. Eldridge had apparently passed over Beverly Axelrod's name for some time before writing her in 1965. When she responded, sympathetic to his problems, and turned out to be feminine—and beautiful besides—the remarkable letters followed.

Who was Beverly Axelrod, aside from being white, a divorcee, and a civil rights lawyer? In the title essay of *Soul on Ice*, written October 9, 1965, Eldridge describes her more completely in what seems to be an attempt to explain his *unconvict-like* affection for *a lawyer*, of all people. He had apparently suffered some indignities because of it, from fellow inmates as well as prison authorities.

". . . what matters is that I have fallen in love with my lawyer! Is that surprising? A convict is expected to have a high regard for *anyone* who comes to his aid . . . But can a convict really love a lawyer? It goes against the grain. Convicts hate lawyers. . . .

". . . It was learned by the convicts that I'd gotten busted with some magazines given to me by my lawyer and that I was thrown in the Hole for it. Convicts smiled knowingly and told me that I had gone for the greasy pig, that my lawyer had set me up, and that if I couldn't see through the plot I was so stupid that I would buy not only the Golden Gate Bridge but fried ice cream. . . .

"It was my turn to smile knowingly. . . . I love my

lawyer. My lawyer is not an ordinary person. My lawyer is a rebel, a revolutionary who is alienated fundamentally from the *status quo*, probably with as great an intensity, conviction, and irretrievability as I am alienated from it—and probably with more intelligence, compassion and humanity. If you read the papers, you are no doubt aware of my lawyer's incessant involvement in agitation against all manifestations of the monstrous evil of our system, such as our intervention in the internal affairs of the Vietnamese people or the invasion of the Dominican Republic by U.S. Marines.

"And my lawyer defends civil rights demonstrators, sit-iners, and the Free Speech students . . . at the University of California. My love for my lawyer is due, in part, to these activities and involvements, because we are always on the same side of the issues. And I love all my allies. . . .

"I suppose that I should be honest and, before going any further, admit that my lawyer is a woman—or maybe I should have held back with that piece of the puzzle—a very excellent, unusual, and beautiful woman. I know that *she* believes that I do not really love her and that I am confusing a combination of lust and gratitude for love. Lust and gratitude I feel abundantly, but I also love this woman. And I fear that, believing that I do not love her, she will act according to that belief. . . ."

Mrs. Axelrod consummated her part of the bargain as a lawyer and worked diligently for the next eighteen months to get Eldridge freed on parole in November, 1966. But the romance was never consummated beyond correspondence. The love affair seems to have died an easy, natural death after his release, lapsing into a friendship that dwindled and at last became separated by the distance which the tense times imposed on both Eldridge and Beverly as each headed toward their separate destinies.

Whatever, the sensibilities and sensitivity Eldridge expressed in the letters has been forgotten—and that is a tragedy. They show a part of him as deep as, if not deeper than the causes of the more evident fury of his Black Panther oratory. The latter arose from his race—his blackness. What he shared in his letters to Beverly was his humanity.

* * * *

How different those letters to Beverly were from other writing which rattled from Eldridge's typewriter in 1965. There was always the rage, but also knife-sharp social criticism, keen political analysis, and even mourning.

Of the dated essays in *Soul on Ice,* the earliest is June 19, 1965. It is Eldridge's reaction to the assassination of Malcolm X which had happened in New York, February 21, almost four months earlier.

Eldridge had been sitting in "the darkened hulk of Mess Hall No. 1—which convicts call 'The Folsom Theater'—watching Victor Buono in . . . *The Strangler . . .*" when a fellow convict named Silly Willie came to him and told him Malcolm X had been shot.

The news stunned Eldridge. "For a moment the earth seemed to reel in orbit. The skin all over my body tightened up," he wrote later.

After the movie ended, Eldridge filed out with the others to see the shocked expression on the faces of inmates in the yard and hear the comments of dismay, sorrow, and revenge.

Eldridge was a Black Muslim at the time, although he admitted later he stumbled over praying to "Allah." He had agreed with Malcolm X when the latter had split away from Elijah Muhammad's leadership.

The Black Muslims were formed back in the thirties by Elijah Poole. He had renamed himself Elijah Muhammad in the pattern the group adopted of divorcing itself totally from having anything—even names—that hinted of any connection with white America. Black Muslim religion descended from Islam, combining that with black folkways and Protestant Christian beliefs. Members referred to themselves also as the "Lost-Found Nation of Islam in the West." At first, in the Depression, they focused their efforts on aiding their unemployed, disinherited black brothers; later they sought complete separation from the white community, advocating establishment of a separate distinct nation within the United States. After a television documentary in 1959, "The Hate That Hate Produced," the organization's membership swelled to something like thirty thousand blacks.

Muslim theology offered a belief in black superiority. The Black Race had been the first and only race, according to Muslim beliefs. A mad scientist named Yakub had rebelled against Allah and later invented the white race, or race of devils. Someday the white man would be destroyed; but until then, blacks must separate and organize their own nation.

However much their theories were founded on

hatred, the Black Muslims were not in their first years usually violent or antisocial. As O'Neill points out in *Coming Apart*, they "avoided tobacco, alcohol, narcotics, and 'soul food' (another relic of slavery). They were frugal and industrious and where possible founded their own schools and businesses. They never got into trouble with the law, except when harassed by it. . . ."

Malcolm X, an ex-convict formerly named Malcolm Little who had educated himself in prison and had joined the Black Muslims to become the brilliant chief spokesman of the party—next to Elijah Muhammad, the party's "Light." He and Elijah Muhammad had had a falling out in 1963-64. Ostensibly it came about from a remark made by Malcolm X about President Kennedy's assassination being a matter of "chickens coming home to roost." Actually its cause was Malcolm's belief that blacks could cooperate with whites safely and to everyone's advantage. This was unheard-of blasphemy against Black Muslim beliefs and so Malcolm X was forced out of the party's mainstream. But he made a pilgrimage to Mecca and a triumphal tour of Africa and the Near East in 1964 and returned in early 1965 to found the Organization of Afro-American Unity and to establish the Muslim Mosque, Inc., which attracted many Black Muslims away from Elijah Muhammad. An unknown assassin's bullet cut him down as he addressed a rally in New York.

Eldridge agreed wholeheartedly with Malcolm X's views and when the rift between Malcolm and Elijah occurred he said so at a secret meeting of Muslims at Folsom. He had urged others to choose between the two black leaders and had persuaded them to follow

Malcolm X. Eldridge's defection from Elijah, the great black "Light," caused a great deal of consternation among the prison's Muslims, because Eldridge himself by that time had become a person of prestige throughout California's prison system as a Muslim leader.

Eldridge had always held on to the hope for some reconciliation. But Malcolm's death "made the split final," Eldridge wrote that June day in 1965, adding, "These events caused a profound personal crisis in my life and beliefs. . . ." It appeared to erase all hopes of the kind of black-white brotherhood Malcolm X had been striving for, as he had written in a letter from the Holy Land on his tour, ". . . I have eaten from the same plate with people whose eyes were the bluest of blue, whose hair was the blondest of blond and whose skin was the whitest of white . . . and I felt the sincerity in the words and deeds of these 'white' Muslims. . . ." It was the same sincerity that he had felt among blacks of Africa. Malcolm X's death was a time of profound mourning for Eldridge.

"Many of us were shocked and outraged" by Malcolm X's letter, Eldridge recalled. ". . . There were those of us who were glad to be liberated from a doctrine of hate and racial supremacy. The onus of teaching racial supremacy and hate, which is the white man's burden, is pretty hard to bear."

His hopes of brotherhood thwarted by Malcolm X's death, Eldridge's mourning turned to rage. He didn't buy the rumors that Malcolm had been assassinated by Muhammad's discontents over the Black Muslim rifts.

"So now Malcolm is no more," he continued June 19. "The bootlickers, Uncle Toms, lackeys and stooges of the white power structure have done their best to denigrate Malcolm, to root him out of his people's heart, to tarnish his memory. But their million-worded lies fall on deaf ears. . . ."

He quoted a section from Ossie Davis' eulogy of Malcolm which included, ". . . Malcolm was our manhood, our living, black manhood! This was his meaning to his people. And in honoring him, we honor the best in ourselves. . . ."

To feel and speak so highly of Malcolm X was at the time to ally yourself with Black Power and Black Revolution capitalized. Despite all his talk about brotherhood, Malcolm X was the personification of black extremism. As William O'Neill in *Coming Apart* describes him, "He was the first black revolutionary. He believed in guns. He put the honky down."

Eldridge's devotion to Malcolm raised eyebrows for other reasons, too. Malcolm's hard line, although softer than Elijah's separatism by his willingness to include whites in his "brotherhood," stemmed from years-old conflict within the black race itself. Many adhered to the conciliatory behavior and cooperativeness of Booker T. Washington. But others followed the more militant opposition of W.E.B. DuBois who directly countered Washington's conciliation saying Washington "apologizes for injustice"; sixty years earlier, back in 1905, DuBois declared, "We will not be satisfied with less than our full manhood rights."

Born in 1868 of French, Dutch and Negro ancestry, DuBois was educated at Fisk and Harvard, getting his Ph.D. from Harvard in 1895. He was teaching economics and history at Atlanta University when he made that militant declaration. He later edited the NAACP's journal, *Crisis*, for a while, and during the

63

Pan-African Conferences in the twenties he led the call for independence of African colonies. During the World War II years he moved from his nonideological radicalism towards Marxist thinking, leading him finally to join the Communist Party-USA in 1961. The next year he sought exile in Africa.

By 1965, many blacks in the civil rights movement were seeking their "full manhood rights" in DuBois' militant sense, but his name was still prominent chiefly for his being the founder of the DuBois Clubs, then considered as the youth affiliation of the Communist Party. DuBois died in 1963, remembered by militant leaders as a leader in their cause.

So when Eldridge in June, 1965, picked up that demand and wrote, out of grief-filled frustration, "We shall have our manhood. We shall have it or the earth will be leveled by our attempts to gain it," the world remembered only his rage, not his sorrow that a hero who hoped for some kind of white-black brotherhood had been cut down.

Then Eldridge forgot his mourning and concentrated on his own rage. On June 25, 1965, in what became the opening pages of his book he wrote of his reactions to the whole segregation controversy that had swirled for twelve years, ". . . I turned away from America with horror, disgust, and outrage.

"In Soledad state prison, I fell in with a group of blacks who, like myself, were in vociferous rebellion against what we perceived as a continuation of slavery on a higher plane. We cursed everything American—including baseball and hot dogs. All respect we may have had for politicians, preachers, lawyers, governors, Presidents, senators, congressmen was utterly destroyed as we watched them temporizing and compromising over right and wrong, over legality and illegality, over constitutionality and unconstitutionality.

"We knew that in the end what they were clashing over was us, what to do with the blacks, and whether or not to start treating us as human beings. I despised all of them."

He let his soul hang out during 1965, not just his heart as in his letters to Beverly Axelrod or in his mourning for Malcolm. In August he wrote about Watts, noting how "Watts was a place of shame," and how many blacks in prison and out "used to use Watts as an epithet in much the same way as city boys used 'country' as a term of derision." But in the aftermath of the July Watts holocaust, Eldridge and others joined in the joy expressed by convicts from Watts.

Eldridge wrote, "It was a cleansing, revolutionary laugh we all shared. . . ."

In September, besides his love letters, Eldridge was also busy writing about his religious experiences, something that flowed into and out of his typewriter in the solitary sanctuary of his cell.

Earlier in June, he had mentioned how the group of young blacks he had joined in Soledad espoused atheism. "Unsophisticated and not based on any philosophical rationale, our atheism was pragmatic. I had come to believe that there is no God; if there is, men do not know anything about Him. Therefore, all religions were phony—which made all preachers and priests, in our eyes, fakers, including the ones scurrying around the prison who, curiously, could put in a good word for you with the Almighty Creator of the

Universe but who could not get anything done with the warden or parole board—they could usher you through the Pearly Gates *after you were dead*, but not through the prison gates *while you were still alive and kicking*.

"Besides, men of the cloth who work in prison have an ineradicable stigma attached to them in the eyes of convicts because they escort condemned men into the gas chamber. Such men of God are powerful arguments in favor of atheism.

"Later on, I bolstered our arguments by reading Thomas Paine and his devastating critique of Christianity in particular and organized religion in general."

Eldridge had mentioned then, in June, that his reading and thinking and espoused atheism led him to become an "extreme iconoclast." Once thinking that, although he didn't know what was happening in the universe, somewhere out there amidst all that humanity some unanimity existed, he was finding in the racial troubles that it didn't. ". . . here I was discovering that the whole U.S.A. was in a chaos of disagreement over segregation/integration."

So he threw everything and everybody to the winds. It gave him a superb sense of freedom to "accept nothing until it was proved that it was good— for me."

It became a game and he got good at it. "I attacked all forms of piety, loyalty, and sentiment: marriage, love, God, patriotism, the Constitution, and founding fathers, law, concepts of right-wrong-good-evil, all forms of ritualized and conventional behavior. . . ."

Then on September 10th, the same day Beverly Axelrod penned her reply to his first love letter, Eldridge let some more of his religious history come out. "Once I was a Catholic. I was baptized, made my first Communion, my Confirmation, and I wore a Cross with Jesus on it around my neck. I prayed at night, said my Rosary, went to Confession, and said all the Hail Marys and Our Fathers to which I was sentenced by the priest.

"Hopelessly enamored of sin myself, yet appalled by the sins of others, I longed for Judgment Day and a trial before a jury of my peers—this was my only chance to escape the flames which I could feel already licking at my feet. I was in a California Youth Authority institution at the time, having transgressed the laws of man—God did not indict me that time; if He did, it was a secret indictment, for I was never informed of any charges brought against me.

"The reason I became a Catholic was that the rule of the institution held that every Sunday each inmate had to attend the church of his choice. I chose the Catholic Church because all the Negroes and Mexicans went there. The whites went to the Protestant chapel. Had I been fool enough to go to the Protestant chapel, one black face in a sea of white, and with guerrilla warfare going on between us, I might have ended up a Christian martyr—St. Eldridge the Stupe.

"It all ended one day," Eldridge wrote, "when at a catechism class, the priest asked if anyone present understood the mystery of the Holy Trinity. I had been studying my lessons diligently and knew by heart what I'd been taught. Up shot my hand, my heart throbbing with piety (pride) for this chance to demonstrate my knowledge of the Word.

"To my great shock and embarrassment, the Father announced, and it sounded like a thunderclap, that I was lying, that no one, not even the Pope, understood the Godhead, and why else did I think they called it the *mystery* of the Holy Trinity?

"I saw in a flash, stung to the quick by the jeers of my fellow catechumens, that I had been used, that the Father had been lying in wait for the chance to drop that thunderbolt, in order to drive home the point that the Holy Trinity was not to be taken lightly.

"I had intended to explain the Trinity with an analogy to 3-in-1 oil, so it was probably just as well."

That same day in September, Eldridge got to thinking about "The Christ" and his teachings. "The Christ" was Chris Lovdjieff, who used to teach classes at San Quentin. Convicts looked to him as a kind of prison guru. He taught on everything, history, philosophy, metaphysics, all the world's religions including Zen and existentialism. He was there all the time, nights and weekends, helping convicts in their thinking about life's BIG questions. His classes were so popular "the officials would sometimes have to send a guard to his class to make him stop teaching, so the inmates could be locked up for the night."

Lovdjieff created an atmosphere "like the mystic spell of Kahlil Gibran's poetry. Lovdjieff was a magnet, an institution. . . . In his classes he was a dictator, . . ." Eldridge wrote, "allowing no smoking by students, other teachers, even visiting guards who came in smoking their pipes." Yet "he burned incense in his classroom when he lectured on religion, to evoke a certain mood. . . ."

He did wonders with the convicts. He gave Eldridge an insatiable appetite for reading, one that ascended far above Eldridge's already highly intelligent curiosity.

When Eldridge was transferred in 1963 from San Quentin to Folsom for being an agitator and put in solitary confinement, he developed the habit—followed in later solitary confinements—of stocking up on piles of books as part of his calisthenics-reading crash program for maintaining sanity while isolated.

And that led Eldridge to read Thomas Merton's *The Seven Storey Mountain*. Although he rejected Merton's "theistic world," he could not keep Merton "out of the room. He shouldered his way through the door. Welcome, Brother Merton. I give him a bear hug. . . ." Merton's description of New York's black ghetto, ". . . this huge, dark, steaming slum . . ." in which ". . . hundreds of thousands of Negroes are herded together like cattle, most of them with nothing to eat and nothing to do . . ." was a constant reminder to Eldridge not to soften under Merton's otherwise tender monasticism. "I had only to read that passage," Eldridge wrote, "to become once more a rigid flame of indignation. It had precisely the same effect on me that Elijah Muhammad's writings used to have, or the words of Malcolm X. . . ."

Lovdjieff, "The Christ" of San Quentin did that for Eldridge. But the time came that they fell out. Lovdjieff had preached one time for a whole week on love, what novelists and playwrights and philosophers had said about love. Then he asked his students to write an essay on how they had been influenced by the week-long teachings.

Eldridge quoted Malcolm X to explain how he could not love white people: "How can I love the man who raped my mother, killed my father, enslaved my ancestors, dropped atomic bombs on Japan, killed off the Indians and keeps me cooped up in the slums? I'd rather be tied up in a sack and tossed into the Harlem River first."

Lovdjieff refused to grade Eldridge's paper. He was stunned and hurt by what Eldridge had written.

" 'How can you do this to me?' he asked.

" 'I've only written the way I feel,' I said.

"Instead of answering, he cried.

" 'Jesus wept,' I told him and walked out.

"Two days later, he returned my essay—ungraded. There were instead spots on it which I realized to be his tears."

One thing Lovdjieff did not do. "The Christ" of San Quentin did not make the Christ of the Bible real to Eldridge. An inferno of years would flame past before that happened. Meantime, there was only rage. As best as he could in prison, Eldridge kept his sanity—or perhaps better, kept himself in shape in order to keep his rage at peak function—by getting up at 5:30 A.M. long before the 7:00 A.M. morning count.

In that early morning time before seven he would make up his bed, clean up his cell, do calisthenics—kneebends, butterflies, touching toes, squats, windmills, pushups—in the nude, take a "jailbird" bath in the little cell sink, shave, and write anything he wanted to go out in the morning mail.

Convicts ate breakfast at 7:30, then went to the day's duties, which for Eldridge consisted of work in the bakery until about noon.

From noon until shortly after 3:00 P.M. was "free" time when prisoners could go back to their cells or to the library or out to the yard to walk or enjoy the sun or play games or get some more exercise. Evening lock-up time was 3:20 P.M. with another head-count at 6:30 P.M.

It went that way for nearly nine years for Eldridge at San Quentin and Folsom, his second and longest prison stint. His first term had begun in Soledad in 1954, when he was eighteen and thus eligible for adult lockup. He had served about two years on that first term before parole, but freedom had been short-lived. What happened during that freedom is perhaps Eldridge's most desperate and most eloquent expression of his rage.

Eldridge let that all hang out in what he wrote June 25, 1965. Entitled, "On Becoming," this piece has haunted me because it shows the depths to which some people go before their soul-searching finally unearths a valuable discovery. For a black man this journey into manhood often encounters strange symbols as obstacles.

In Soledad, as an iconoclast who derided everything, demanding proof of everything until he decided it was "good—for me," Eldridge "pranced about, club in hand, seeking new idols to smash. . . .

". . . I encountered really for the first time in my life, with any seriousness, The Ogre, rising up before me in a mist. I discovered, with alarm, that The Ogre possessed a tremendous and dreadful power over me, and I didn't understand this power or why I was at its mercy.

"I tried to repudiate The Ogre, root it out of my heart as I had done God, Constitution, principles, morals, and values—but The Ogre had its claws buried in the core of my being and refused to let go. I fought frantically to be free, but The Ogre only mocked me and sank its claws

71

deeper into my soul. I knew then that I had found an important key, that if I conquered The Ogre and broke its power over me I would be free. But I also knew that it was a race against time and that if I did not win I would certainly be broken and destroyed.

"I, a black man, confronted The Ogre—the white woman."

Convicts have a bad time with sex, since they are isolated from its normal expression. Eldridge faced his problem his way. Confronting The Ogre, he cut out his, a pin-up girl from the *Esquire* and pasted it up on the wall of his cell.

It was a short romance though. "I married a voluptuous bride. Our marriage went along swell for a time: no quarrels, no complaints. And then, one evening when I came in from school, I was shocked and enraged to find that the guard had entered my cell, ripped my sugar from the wall, torn her into little pieces, and left the pieces floating in the commode: it was like seeing a dead body floating in a lake. Giving her a proper burial, I flushed the commode. As the saying goes, I sent her to Long Beach.

"But I was genuinely beside myself with anger: almost every cell, excepting those of the homosexuals, had a pin-up girl on the wall and the guards didn't bother them. Why, I asked the guard the next day, had he singled me out for special treatment?"

He asked the guard and got an insult for an answer. There were rules against pasting pictures on the prison walls; they were generally overlooked. But Eldridge had overstepped the bounds of such winking at rules. Still, the guard would continue to wink, if. . . .

" 'Tell you what,' " the guard smiled at Eldridge,

putting him on guard, " 'I'll compromise with you: get yourself a colored girl for a pin-up—no white women—and I'll let it stay up. Is that a deal?'

"I was more embarrassed than shocked. He was laughing in my face," Eldridge recalled.

The incident made Eldridge face The Ogre by talking about white women to other blacks to see how they felt. Feelings were mixed but by far they wanted nothing black but "a Cadillac." Black women were excommunicated from black idol-worship.

The discussions never ended and Eldridge and his inmate colleagues finally came to notice, ". . . how thoroughly, as a matter of course, a black growing up in America is indoctrined with the white race's standard of beauty. Not that whites made a conscious, calculated effort to do this, we thought, but since they constituted the majority the whites brainwashed the blacks by the very processes the whites employed to indoctrinate themselves with their own group standards.

"It intensified my frustrations to know that I was indoctrinated to see the white woman as more beautiful than my own black woman. . . ."

This had persisted during those first months in Soledad until 1955 when Emmett Till, a young Chicago black visiting in Mississippi, was murdered for allegedly flirting with a white woman. He had been shot, his head crushed from repeated blows with a blunt instrument and his weighted, decomposed body later fished from the river. Eldridge was understandably angered.

Then ". . . . one day I saw in a magazine a picture of the white woman with whom Emmett Till was said to have flirted. While looking at the picture, I felt that little tension in the center of my chest I experience when a woman appeals to me. I was disgusted and angry with myself.

"Here was a woman who had caused the death of a black, possibly because, when he looked at her, he also felt the same tensions of lust and desire in his chest. . . . I looked at the picture again and again, and in spite of everything and against my will and the hate I felt for the woman and all that she represented, she appealed to me. I flew into a rage at myself, at America, at white women, at the history that had placed those tensions . . . in my chest.

"Two days later, I had a 'nervous breakdown.' For several days I ranted and raved against the white race, against white women in particular, against white America in general. When I came to myself, I was locked in a padded cell with not even the vaguest memory of how I got there."

He had several sessions with a prison psychiatrist who came to the remarkable conclusion that Eldridge hated his mother. But he wouldn't listen to any of Eldridge's talk about America's racial problems. Only when Eldridge quit his "diatribes against the whites" was he let out of the hospital.

Though he went back into the general prison routine without any problems, he continued to brood. One thing which took his mind off black men and The Ogre was his introduction to Karl Marx and socialism. It was diverting, but instead of capitalism becoming his enemy as it was Marx's, the white woman became his target.

". . . Somehow I arrived at the conclusion that, as a matter of principle, it was of paramount importance for me to have an antagonistic, ruthless attitude toward white women. The term *outlaw* appealed to me and at the time my parole date was drawing near, 1 considered myself to be mentally free—I was an 'outlaw.' I had stepped outside of the white man's law, which I repudiated with scorn and self-satisfaction. I became a law unto myself. . . ."

Paroled in 1956, "I became a rapist. . . ."

It was the ultimate expression of rage.

* * * *

Then twenty-one, and with two and a half years of adult prison preceded by several earlier years in reform school under his belt, Eldridge now began a short but shocking period of his life.

In a long profile on Eldridge in the November 16, 1968, issue of the *Saturday Evening Post*, Don A. Schanche said, Eldridge "worked hard at his sales business and raped on weekends."

In *Soul*, Eldridge himself confessed, "To refine my technique and *modus operandi*, I started out by practicing on black girls in the ghetto—in the black ghetto where dark and vicious deeds appear not as aberrations or deviations from the norm, but as part of the sufficiency of the Evil of a day—and when I considered myself smooth enough, I crossed the tracks and sought out white prey.

"I did this consciously, deliberately, willfully, methodically—though looking back I see that I was in a frantic, wild, and completely abandoned frame of mind.

"Rape was an insurrectionary act. It delighted me that I was defying and trampling upon the white man's law, upon his system of values, and that I was defiling his women—and this point, I believe, was the most satisfying to me because I was very resentful over the historical fact of how the white man has used the black woman.

"I felt I was getting revenge. From the site of the act of rape, consternation spreads outwardly in concentric circles. I wanted to send waves of consternation throughout the white race. . . .

". . . I know that if I had not been apprehended I would have slit some white throats. There are, of course, many young blacks out there right now who are slitting white throats and raping the white girl . . ." Eldridge wrote on June 25th some eight years later.

Eldridge enjoyed eleven months of freedom in 1956-57 to work out his revenge in such insurrectionary acts before being apprehended. His arrest, according to one Alameda County deputy district attorney who confessed he didn't have all the details, "had something to do" with Eldridge's grabbing a nurse in the parking lot of a Los Angeles hospital. When people came to help her, he started shooting as he made his getaway. "No one was hit as I remember," said the deputy D.A. Eldridge was charged with rape, two counts of assault with intent to commit murder, and three counts of assault with a deadly weapon.

The rape charges were dropped, but on March 20, 1958, according to the records, Eldridge was sentenced on the other charges. The terms were to run concurrently. The assault with intent to commit murder charge was the greater offense and so that took precedence—up to fourteen years in prison. He was sent to San Quentin. When he wrote the shocking details on that Friday night in 1965, he was into his eighth year of the sentence.

The "abandoned frame of mind" which had sent him amok had long since disappeared.

"After I returned to prison," he continued writing, "I took a long look at myself and, for the first time in my life, admitted that I was wrong, that I had gone astray—astray not so much from the white man's law as from being human, civilized—for I could not approve the act of rape.

"Even though I had some insight into my own motivations, I did not feel justified. I lost my self-respect. My pride as a man dissolved and my whole fragile moral structure seemed to collapse, completely shattered.

"That is why I started to write. To save myself. (Italics mine.)

"I realized that no one could save me but myself. The prison authorities were both uninterested and unable to help me. I had to seek out the truth and unravel the snarled web of my motivations. I had to find out who I am and what I want to be, what type of man I should be, and what I could do to become the best of which I was capable.

"I understood that what had happened to me had also happened to countless other blacks and it would happen to many, many more.

"I learned that I had been taking the easy way out, running away from problems. I also learned that it is easier to do evil than it is to do good.

"And I have been terribly impressed by the youth of America, black and white. I am proud of them because they have reaffirmed my faith in humanity. I have come to feel what must be love for the young people of America and I want to be part of the good and greatness that they want for all people. From my prison cell, I have watched America slowly coming awake. It is not fully awake yet, but there is soul in the air and everywhere I see beauty.

"I have watched the sit-ins, the freedom raids, the Mississippi Blood Summers, demonstrations all over the country, the FSM movement, the teach-ins, and the mounting protest over Lyndon Strangelove's foreign policy—all of this, the thousands of little details, show me it is time to straighten up and fly right.

"That is why I decided to concentrate on my writing and efforts in this area. We are a very sick country—I, perhaps, am sicker than most. But I accept that. . . .

"I was very familiar with the Eldridge who came to prison, but that Eldridge no longer exists. And the one I am now is in some ways a stranger to me. You may find this difficult to understand but it is very easy for one in prison to lose his sense of self. And if he has been undergoing all kinds of extreme, involved, and unregulated changes, then he ends up not knowing who he is. . . .

"Individuality is not nourished in prison, neither by the officials nor by the convicts. It is a deep hole out of which to climb."

It all poured out. Bold confession. Repentance. Reaffirmation. Identity search. And then, purpose:

"What must be done, I believe, is that all these problems—particularly the sickness between the white woman and the black man—must be brought out into the open, dealt with and resolved. I know that the black man's sick attitude toward the white woman is a revolutionary sickness: it keeps him perpetually out of harmony with the system that is oppressing him.

"Many whites flatter themselves with the idea that the Negro male's lust and desire for the white dream girl is purely an esthetic attraction, but nothing could be farther from the truth.

"His motivation is often of such a bloody, hateful, bitter, and malignant nature that whites would really be hard pressed to find it flattering.

"I have discussed these points with prisoners who were convicted of rape, and their motivations are very plain. But they are very reluctant to discuss these things with white men who, by and large, make up the prison staffs. I believe that in the experience of these men lies the knowledge and wisdom that must be utilized to help other youngsters who are heading in the same direction. I think all of us, the entire nation, will be better off if we bring it all out front. A lot of people's feelings will be hurt, but that is the price that must be paid.

"It may be that I can harm myself by speaking frankly and directly, but I do not care about that at all. Of course I want to get out of prison, badly, but I shall get out some day. I am more concerned with what I am going to be after I get out. I know that by following the course which I have charted, I will find my salvation.

"If I had followed the path laid down for me by the officials, I'd undoubtedly have long since been out of prison—but I'd be less of a man. I'd be weaker and less certain of where I want to go, what I want to do, and how to go about it.

"The price of hating other human beings is loving oneself less."

People remembered Eldridge's writing that, but let the fact that he was a rapist overshadow their memories of the insight. How unfortunate! He *was* a rapist, yes, but he was also concerned with values and costs. He had written to Beverly Axelrod that the price of loving is allowing oneself to become vulnerable. His rapist period made him aware of the cost of hating others. There would be a price to pay for his soul-searching, too. Too often, the cost of confession is to be misunderstood. In confessing himself in *Soul on Ice*, Eldridge made himself vulnerable before the whole world.

At the risk of belaboring this part of Eldridge's life, I want to mention another essay in *Soul*, the last in the book, which strikes me as giving much insight as to how deep the reaches of the human soul really are.

The essay, "To All Black Women, From All Black Men," is undated. Eldridge begins as though addressing a letter: "Queen—Mother—Daughter of Africa, Sister of my Soul, Black Bride of My Passion, My Eternal Love. I greet you, my Queen, not in the obsequious whine of a cringing Slave to which you have become accustomed, neither do I greet you in . . . the unctuous supplications of the sleek Black Bourgeoise, nor the bullying bellow of the rude Free Slave—but in my own voice do I greet you, the voice of the Black Man. . . .

"I have Returned from the dead. I speak to you now from the Here and Now. I was dead for four hundred years. For four hundred years you have been a woman alone, bereft of her man . . ."

". . . . Across the naked abyss of negated masculinity, . . . we face each other today my Queen. I feel a deep, terrifying hurt, the pain of humiliation. . . . I feel unjustified. I can't bear to look into your eyes . . . I tremble inside each time you look at me. . . .

"My Queen, it is hard for me to tell you what is in my heart for you today—what is in the heart of all my black brothers for you and all your black sisters—and I fear I will fail unless you reach out to me, tune in on me with the antenna of your love, the sacred love in ultimate degree which you were unable to give me because I, being dead, was unworthy to receive it. . . .

"Let me drink from the river of your love at its source, let the lines of force of your love seize my soul by its core and heal the wound of my Castration. . . . Flower of Africa, it is only through the liberating power of your re-love that my manhood can be redeemed. For it is in your eyes, before you, that my need is to be justified. Only, only, only you and only you can condemn or set me free. . . .

"*I have died the ninth death of the cat, have seen Satan face to face and turned my back on God, and have dined in the Swine's Trough, and descended to the uttermost echelon of the Pit, have entered the Den and seized my—from the teeth of a roaring lion!*

". . . I, the Black Eunuch . . . walked the earth with my mind locked in Cold Storage. . . . Black woman, without asking how, just say that we survived our forced march and travail through the Valley of Slavery, Suffering, and Death—there, that Valley there beneath us hidden by that drifting mist. Ah, what sights and sounds and pain lie beneath that mist! . . .

"But put on your crown, my Queen, and we will build a New City on these ruins."

"To All Black Women From All Black Men" is certainly an appropriate title. But the content goes beyond the title. Eldridge seems to speak not only to all black women—to the Black Female Idol, apologizing and confessing his (and black men's) sin of neglect and faithlessness in preferring the white woman—The Ogre—to her, but he speaks to and for all men and women. There is something universal in that heart cry of anguish, in all that recognition of wrongdoing, that confession and promise of better behavior. His release of anguish is identical with the soul-cry heard down through the centuries since Adam.

As Paul wrote to the Christians in Corinth, "For what man knoweth the things of a man, save the spirit of man which is in him?" Every person should be able to recognize Eldridge's spirit expressing itself. There is a deeper symbolism than the one Eldridge was aware of using—deeper than the Black Queen-Mother-Sister-Bride. She was the idol, but such an idol, so all-encompassing, as to be a god—God Himself.

If that's so, and Eldridge's spirit was really crying out to God, then God was at work in Eldridge there in his cell pounding away at his typewriter in 1965.

This will seem like foolish talk to many, but those who have been born again, who have gone, alone because the trip is always solitary, up the hill to the cross, will understand. Who is to say God does not serve out prison terms with convicts? We admit God to be omnipresent, everywhere at all times.

The language Eldridge used in that final essay is filled with biblical vocabulary. Not only in that one essay, but in all of his writings, similar language, similar references and images can be seen. His favorite term for America became "Babylon." He constantly dealt with universal, basic issues. Much more came out of Eldridge before he found out, as he said he was determined to do, ". . . who I am and what I want to be, what type of man I should be, and what I could do to become the best of which I was capable."

The essay "To All Black Women" is not that far out; it is just another piece, fitting in with everything else he wrote in jail and after, of the fabric that was to become the Eldridge Cleaver who was to "send waves of consternation throughout the white race" not only during the raging sixties but even after he descended from the plane at Kennedy Airport into the arms of FBI agents—and ever since, even up to now.

And when I say I think God was there in that Folsom prison cell with Eldridge, and that He was working on Eldridge, I don't imply, even slightly, that Eldridge was a saint, called differently from any other man and woman, for a special significance or purpose. God is with each person at all times and all places, endeavoring to reveal himself one more time, just as He has done throughout the Bible. He was in that jail cell with Eldridge.

Eldridge though, determined to go it alone. He had become an iconoclast, disavowing everything and everyone, in his Soledad years. So he set out on his Ogre trip, got knocked down, came back more determinedly after "my pride as a man dissolved and my whole fragile moral structure seemed to collapse, completely shattered," to "save myself . . ." he wrote. Another instance of man realizing his troubles but not sensing God's everlasting prodding. So Eldridge poked through the rubble of his soul, letting everything hang out. He emerged from the exploratory surgery a more compassionate, concerned man—but so fiercely determined that he expressed himself in the rage of the times.

Soul on Ice is a burningly frigid book, but it is the breaking up of Eldridge's inner ice jam. And like all ice jams blocking strong, flowing currents, it burst loose with destructive force. That—destruction—is what the world saw in Eldridge. But what *Soul on Ice* really is, is a melting. The early signs of spring thaw. The melting of a man's soul. But before the currents were to flow smoothly again, the breakup threatened destruction.

* * * *

What lay behind the ice jam? How did Eldridge reach that convict-essayist stage of his life? Where had he come from to begin the destructive breakup which would make him such a frightening part of his times in the frightened world of the 1960s?

CHAPTER TWO

BOY AND MAN

Leroy Eldridge Cleaver was born in Little Rock, Arkansas, on a Saturday in the middle of the Depression, August 31, 1935. He was the first son born to Leroy and Thelma Cleaver. In the light of later years there is irony in the fact that, on that same day, Congress passed the First Neutrality Act, prohibiting the shipment of U.S. arms to warring nations—being neutral was never to be part of Eldridge's nature.

Being beyond the fringes of the Deep South, the Cleavers escaped the worst ravages which Negroes suffered during those poverty-torn years, particularly since Leroy was a waiter and pianist and his wife a grade school teacher. To be sure, these jobs didn't pay much at that time, but at least they were jobs that paid income. Thousands of other blacks were not so fortunate. For a while Leroy was accompanist in a Little Rock night club for an up-and-coming singer named Dick Powell, before Powell went on to fame and fortune in Hollywood.

With five children the Cleavers couldn't chance the

risks of Hollywood, so they stayed on in Arkansas. Within a few years the family worked its way up even further into the black middle class when Leroy got a job as a dining car waiter on the Santa Fe Super Chief between Los Angeles and Chicago. Eldridge's mother was pregnant with the last child when the family moved to Phoenix, one of his father's drop-off points on the Super Chief's run, to stay together.

Both of Eldridge's grandfathers were Baptist preachers. This, despite their frequent arguments, gave the family an additional measure of stability. Both parents had jobs in the midst of economic havoc. Mother saw to it that the children received all the educational basics and that they were taught the Bible and sent regularly to Sunday school. But being black in white America generates stresses that affect even the most stable of families.

Most obvious, of course, is that kids grow up aware, as Eldridge would one day include in *Soul on Ice*, that "From the beginning, America has been a schizophrenic nation. Its two conflicting images of itself were never reconciled."

Worse, blacks can never escape that awareness. Knowing about a hurricane is one thing—you can always turn your attention elsewhere. Being in the midst of the maelstrom, though, you have to deal with it every instant.

Dealing with the national schizophrenia was part of Eldridge's heritage. He had less to do with the more noble statements about the unalienable rights of life, liberty and pursuit of happiness. These were all part of the baggage tucked into his kit bag at birth. Fortunately, the biblical heritage was packed in, too.

* * * *

Eldridge got his first taste of the streets in Phoenix. His job as a shoeshine boy required two things for success: customers, and ways to "avoid paying off the police for the privilege of working on his knees" on the city's sidewalks.

"The police had a kind of racket," Eldridge told a *Saturday Evening Post* writer, Don A. Schanche, in 1968, recalling the Phoenix days. "You had to check out your box from the police station (daily) and pay them off. Some of us made our own boxes, and when the police caught us shining shoes, they'd take us in and take our boxes away. So I had to hide mine from them, and I had to hide it from my father, too. He thought that shining shoes was undignified."

Schanche also wrote about "the saddening incident that gave Eldridge his first full awareness of the peculiar relationship of black people to white people."

As Eldridge told it, "It was a public sports contest run for us by white people, and they made a big thing of announcing that there would be prizes for running and jumping and other sports. Prizes are exciting to little kids, and we ran our hearts out. The prize was a piece of watermelon. For really the first time I understood what white people expected of us."

After about two years the Cleavers moved from Phoenix to Los Angeles. Eldridge was about ten at the time and the world was just recuperating from World War II.

"My mother always said I got into trouble because we moved to California," Eldridge tells people today. "I never got into any trouble back in Arkansas." He was also a very little boy back in Arkansas.

From the street wisdom gained with Phoenix police and from the watermelon incident, he began to develop a "real hatred" during the early years in Los Angeles. Eldridge says, "First of all, for those white people whom I considered to be responsible for those things in society that I didn't like. I had a particular attitude towards policemen, political leaders, school officials—and I really didn't have much respect for preachers."

Eldridge's attitudes toward all symbols of authority and largely white authority hardened gradually, but his first overt expression of them came apparently when he got into trouble over some vandalism, then thefts, at the Abraham Lincoln Junior High School.

The school's student population came largely from Rose Hills, near south Pasadena, a mixed neighborhood heavily laden with black families, with a reputation for being the marijuana capital of California. Following a period of friction after the move from Phoenix, Eldridge's mother and father had separated, adding something new to the burden of a black American youngster who already had particular attitudes towards a good part of society. Now he lost the privilege of having his mother and father under the same roof.

Abraham Lincoln Junior High School was integrated, but largely black. The school would graduate Eldridge, not into high school, but into Juvenile Hall and reform school.

Years later, when making a speech in San Francisco, he would tell the audience that Lincoln Junior High was where his crime career started. ". . . At about the age of twelve. . . . I don't know what the charge was—vandalism. I think I ripped off a bicycle, maybe two or three bicycles. Maybe I had a bicycle business, I don't remember. But it related to bicycles. They took me to Juvenile Hall."

Eldridge spent several months in Juvenile Hall before being released. The time was just long enough to put him in contact with a lot of other black youths just like himself. Not only did this give a feeling of solidarity, but it provided a training ground. Others were into vandalism, theft, burglaries and robberies, just as he was, but many were into selling marijuana. Pot-pushing was then a much more horrendous crime than it is today and not nearly so common.

As well as being known as the state's marijuana capital Rose Hills also had a reputation for its big aggressive football players. Kids wanting to work their way out of poverty had two avenues open: play football and hopefully earn a college scholarship and maybe even future fame as a pro, or hustle pot and earn a living in all the many varieties of ghetto crime.

Eldridge tried both. By the time he graduated into Belmont Hill High School, he was almost as big as his eventual six-feet-two and weighed nearly two hundred pounds. He had also grown in his efficiency as a criminal. Another term, this at the Fred C. Nelles School for Boys at Whittier for burglary, had improved his pot-pushing abilities.

At Belmont High he turned out simultaneously for football and hurried back into hustling the weed. Both ventures wound up in failure. A few days before the season's opening game, he was busted for selling pot and shipped off to a new reform school—the Preston School of Industry. He left behind him at home a brand new pair of football shoes he had bought in eager anticipation of his other career. His mother kept the shoes around for years afterwards in a bureau drawer.

The Preston School of Industry had a reputation among those familiar with it quite different from its name. It was a "school for crime." Its education was just the reverse of its publicly avowed principles and purposes.

Discrepancies exist between accounts of Eldridge's shift from Preston to Soledad State Prison. Some writers say that his term in Preston overlapped his eighteenth birthday after which he was transferred to Soledad. Others say he was released from Preston after a brief stay only to be arrested again, this time after he had turned eighteen in August, 1953, and as an adult he was sent to Soledad, June 18, 1954, for two and a half years.

Whatever, Eldridge's eighteenth year was notable. His prison term at Soledad began one month after the U.S. Supreme Court outlawed school segregation. When the full impact of this ruling struck home, he would write in *Soul on Ice*, "I was soon aflame over my newly discovered social status, and inwardly I turned away from America with horror, disgust and outrage."

Earlier, he had turned away from church and had all those "particular attitudes" towards police, politicians, preachers, and school officials. The years in between had hardened his views so that in the years following 1954 he put almost all of society behind him. White society, that is.

Eldridge also repeatedly refers to his eighteenth

year as "the year somebody gave me the *Communist Manifesto* by Karl Marx and Friedrich Engels." This offered him "a blueprint" of the kind of social order he was coming to believe should exist. Obviously Marx's theories didn't explode on his mind all laid out and clear, but Marx was a catalyst in developing Eldridge's outlook.

At a Christian Writers' press conference in January, 1977, he explained this in some detail to reporters: "I had by that time [at eighteen] developed a lot of the very rebellious attitudes, based on my understanding of social, economic, political and racial problems that we had in the country, so I just gave myself over totally to antisocial and misguided rebellion.

"The Marxist ideology for many years seemed to answer all the questions that I had. . . ."

He also explained this in *Soul*. "During this period I was concentrating my reading in the field of economics. Having previously dabbled in the theories and writings of Rousseau, Thomas Paine, and Voltaire, I had added a little polish to my iconoclastic stance, without, however, bothering too much to understand their affirmative positions . . ."

By that he meant that because so many writers saw fit to comdemn Marx, "I sought out his books, and although he kept me with a headache, I took him for my authority. . . . It was like taking medicine for me to find that, indeed, American capitalism deserved all the hatred and contempt that I felt for it in my heart."

This particular period came during Eldridge's battle with The Ogre, and it "had a positive, stabilizing effect upon me—to an extent because I was not about to become stable—and it diverted me from my previous preoccupation: morbid broodings on the black man and the white woman."

He read also, ". . . with very little understanding, some of the passionate, exhortatory writings of Lenin; and I fell in love with Bakunin and Nechayev's *Catechism of the Revolutionist*—the principles of which, along with some of Machiavelli's advice, I sought to incorporate into my own behavior.

"I took the *Catechism* for my bible and, standing on a one-man platform that had nothing to do with the reconstruction of society, I began consciously incorporating these principles into my daily life, to employ tactics of ruthlessness in my dealings with everyone with whom I came into contact. And I began to look at white America through these new eyes."

By 1965, he had gone through enough of such personal, emotional, mental and prison behavior experiences to where he had become (relatively) a model prisoner. He was one of the seasoned veterans whom authorities turned to at times for help with other inmates. The best proof of his weathering was that he was one of the privileged inmates of the honor block at Folsom.

But he was also something more. Blessed with his high degree of intelligence and writing talent, plus the surging inner drives of a healthy, powerful six-foot-two black man, he was ready to emerge into society as an aggressive, influential voice of black revolutionary America.

As Maxwell Geismar was to write in his introduction to *Soul on Ice*, "Eldridge . . . is one of the distinctive new literary voices to be heard. [He] is simply one of the best cultural critics now writing. . . ."

92

Others—police, politicians, FBI Director J. Edgar Hoover, and plain citizens, black and white—would say, ". . . a threat to America," and would shudder at the name of Eldridge Cleaver.

But other blacks and whites, allied with the militancy personified in the Black Panther Party, would call him ". . . the most eloquent spokesman for the Black cause in America today."

CHAPTER THREE

PANTHER

Eldridge's hectic writing at Folsom in 1965 included far more than his soul-searching essays and love letters to Beverly Axelrod. He smuggled some of his writings out of prison via Beverly, who had become his attorney. She successfully secured his release on parole in November, 1966, after negotiating with authorities for nearly eighteen months.

By then it was clearly apparent to him that America's civil rights turmoil was only part of the greater world-wide struggle for the liberation of black peoples. Also clear was that a great gap had developed between the younger generation and their elders. This was becoming evident to Americans, but Eldridge saw the split, too, as world-wide.

Some of his essays in *Soul on Ice* are not dated, and so they may have been written either in prison or shortly after his release while working with the book's publisher; but in these his expanded world views are clearly stated.

In one, "The White Race and Its Heroes," he

declared that "the white race has lost its heroes," not only in America but everywhere. George Washington and Thomas Jefferson had been slave owners, and "Even Winston Churchill, who is looked upon by older whites as perhaps the greatest hero of the twentieth century—even he, because of the system of which he was a creature and which he served, is an arch-villain in the eyes of the young white rebels."

As he reviewed the twelve years of the American civil rights movement, 1954-66, he saw something even more profound and startling: ". . . there has surfaced a political conflict between the generations that is deeper, even, than the struggle between the races." It had started first among Negroes themselves, "when college students in the South, fed up with Uncle Tom's hat-in-hand approach to revolution, threw off the yoke of the NAACP." When those black students started their sit-ins, this spirit of youth-elder rebellion spread across the country and infected thousands of white students, too.

So, by the time he was released in 1966, Eldridge felt that it was "among the white youth of the world that the greatest change is taking place. It is they who are experiencing the great psychic pain of waking into consciousness to find their inherited heroes turned by events into villains."

The younger generation whites, Eldridge felt, had moved from an initial rejection of the kind of conformity their elders expected to where they became convinced that the whole world, and particularly America, "was unacceptable to them in its present form and began an active search" for new roles they should play. That led to white youths joining black demonstrators in growing numbers. But even this was changing to something else by 1966, "a fourth stage, now in its infancy," in which young whites, using the techniques they had learned in their participation in the black struggle, began to "attack problems in the general society." Thus the antiwar, anti-Establishment sentiments which made up the new cause that joined the civil rights movement by the mid-sixties.

America had been "schizophrenic from the beginning" in Eldridge's eyes, and there was "no common ground between these two contradictory images" held by parents and children. Eldridge's faith was in the younger generation, and so in 1966 on his release, he began encouraging them, stirring them to even greater convictions that their parents were totally and horribly wrong, and had been for generations.

He wrote, "There is in America today a generation of white youth that is truly worthy of a black man's respect, and this is a rare event in the foul annals of American history. . . . If a man like Malcolm X could change and repudiate racism, if I myself and other former Muslims can change, if young whites can change, then there is hope for America.

"It was certainly strange to find myself, while steeped in the doctrine that all whites were devils by nature, commanded by the heart to applaud and acknowledge respect for these young whites—despite the fact that they are descendants of the masters and I the descendant of a slave."

That was his frame of mind when he left prison. That was the message he preached, although he confounded millions of people by his use of Marxist language—"capitalist," "oppressor," "imperialist," and the like. Still, he felt those words were better than his former vocabulary which included calling white men "white devils." He felt that everybody was happier with his new, less wild-eyed, stance.

And so, in November, 1966, after being sent back to Soledad, he walked out of prison essentially a free man—free, on parole, but free of prison. If some people seemed "happier" with his new language, many others would not be, and even those happier ones would find that the paroled Eldridge Cleaver was as radically dissident a man as ever. After all, he was still black, and the times were moving toward black revolution. Eldridge himself, although he did not realize it as he left the prison walls behind him, was moving toward the Black Panthers.

* * * *

Eldridge, at thirty-one, was now in the most unique position of his life.

Ramparts magazine, although still in its more orthodox Catholic laymen days was willing to hire him as a reporter. He was also experienced enough to know that he had to live a life far more normal than he had in his pot-pushing, insurrectionist days. Most significantly, he was on the verge of fame, although still over a year away from it—his prison writings were under consideration for publication in book form. *Soul on Ice* would catapult him into national attention and literary immortality.

Eldridge's entry to the *Ramparts'* editorial staff came through Beverly Axelrod who had been busy with those of Eldridge's manuscripts which she had smuggled out of prison for him. In *The New York Times Magazine* September 7, 1969 Harvey Swados wrote of how Eldridge and *Ramparts* met.

"Edward Keating, the West Coast Catholic layman who was one of the founders of *Ramparts*, recalls meeting Miss Axelrod at an anti-Vietnam War rally in the summer of 1965. 'I've got a client who's a would-be writer,' she said, and she handed Keating a pile of manuscript 'about an inch and a half high' to read over the weekend. He found the writing flawed but impressive, and suggested that Miss Axelrod bring her client around for an editorial discussion. 'That won't be easy,' she replied. 'He's in Folsom prison.'

"Keating, himself a lawyer and the first editor to work with Cleaver, went to Folsom to meet him. 'I thought him a very powerful writer, and I was curious as to what he'd be like. This great big, black man walked up, and my very first impression was on how gentle his handshake was. We made small talk about books for a while—I'd brought him some—but he was clearly excited that I cared about his writing.'

"Keating cared enough to send some of it East, to Maxwell Geismar, Thomas Merton, Norman Mailer and John Howard Griffin. Their enthusiastic response was transmitted to the authorities, but it was not until November, 1966 that Cleaver was paroled. By then he had already written most of the pieces—social commentary, letters, polemics—which were to make him a national figure when gathered together in 'Soul on Ice.' "

With the support of such respectable people, and a recent prison background of behavior good enough to have put him in the privileged honor block, the authorities felt safe enough to let Eldridge out on parole. At worst they felt he might become another of the angry black writers then cropping up with increasing frequency.

So, on his release in late 1966, Eldridge showed he was sincere at rehabilitating himself by joining the *Ramparts* staff as a reporter, buying a Volvo station wagon on the installment plan, paying his rent on time, and even opening a savings account. And, of course, he made sure he made all the required visits to his parole officer, like his rent and car payments, on time.

* * * *

As good as freedom was and as promising as his future seemed, Eldridge walked into the fresh air outside prison walls with a lot of anxieties. His outlook on life, as his prison writings attest, was a turbulent one, churning with inner pressures. Also, he was still suffering from his split with the Black Muslims and even more shattered by the assassination of Malcolm X. Not only did he consider the Muslim movement a lost cause, but he now found that Malcolm X's organizations—the Organization of Afro-American Unity and the Muslim Mosque, Inc.—had died with their leader.

So parole cut Eldridge loose from almost all of the foundations of his life of the past nine years. He was a solitary, lonely figure, adrift not only in the way most convicts are when first regaining freedom but in that he was pushed and pulled from within by his deep human concerns—the needs of blacks and whites—of *people*. Most important, he was still *black*, in a world where *black* had already become a frightening word headlined in the nation's press almost minute by minute as the

99

latest racial strife unfolded.

Being loose in that world was far different from being separated from it and observing it from behind prison walls. Eldridge now had to sort out the myriad pieces floating in the swirling social currents while swirling along with them. One wonders whether in some ways he had not been freer in prison. After all, in 1966, he was thirty-one, and had spent half of his life behind bars. He was a stranger in the world beyond them.

Still, Eldridge had tremendous pent-up energy which he used to make this heavy adjustment. Almost immediately he plunged into action designed to do something about the problems he saw. The third week in December, 1966, he met Marvin Jackmon, a black writer who had gained attention for a poem he had written after the Watts holocaust entitled, "Burn Baby, Burn!" and a play entitled *Flowers for the Trashman*. Jackmon was the first person Eldridge tied in with after his release. By January, 1967, they had set up the Black House in San Francisco, a non-Establishment black cultural center. By March, the Black House had become a center for black culture throughout the Bay Area.

At the same time Eldridge was trying to revive a loyal following in Malcolm X's Organization of Afro-American Unity (OAAU). The OAAU effort flopped miserably, but before it did Eldridge put forth what he thought would be a dramatic effort to bring the organization back to life. As part of a larger overall plan to coordinate the total black community in three days of mass action in commemoration of the fourth anniversary of Malcolm X's assassination, Eldridge's plan was to have a convention in San Francisco to found the Bay Area branch of OAAU. Since part of the overall community plan was to have Betty Shabazz, Malcolm X's widow, deliver the memorial's keynote address at a mass meeting in the Bayview Community Center at Hunter's Point (one of San Francisco's two black ghettoes, this near the U.S. naval shipyards south of the city), Eldridge wanted Sister Shabazz to install the new OAAU officers to be elected at the convention.

He put forth his idea in January, but by February it was already being torn apart. The eventual watered-down version of his scheme was a farce as far as he was concerned. But February was to be far more important to Eldridge than he ever dreamed.

One night he attended one of the weekly meetings of the loose coalition called the Bay Area Grass-roots Organizations Planning Committee which was spearheading the Malcolm X Memorial. They met in a dingy little storefront on Scott Street in the Fillmore district, the heart of San Francisco's other black ghetto. The early part of the evening was spent with Eldridge listening to more criticism of his idea for an OAAU convention. He felt the criticism was as much due to his being a newcomer to San Francisco, and thus outside the "established" black community, as it was to the plan itself. Since he was originally from Los Angeles, he had been paroled to San Francisco to assure better rehabilitation in a totally new environment, and thus was a kind of interloper in local affairs.

Part way through all the palavering, though, the room fell quiet. Then he heard the front door lock click and the shuffle of approaching footsteps. He whirled around, thinking the police were invading the meeting—and came face to face for the first time with the Black Panthers.

101

"I fell in love . . . immediately upon my first encounter; it was literally love at first sight," he wrote later.

"I spun around in my seat and saw the most beautiful sight I had ever seen: four black men wearing black berets, powder blue shirts, black leather jackets, black trousers, shiny black shoes—and each with a gun! In front was Huey P. Newton with a riot pump shotgun in his right hand, barrel pointed down to the floor. Beside him was Bobby Seale, the handle of a .45-caliber automatic showing from its holster on his right hip, just below the hem of his jacket. A few steps behind Seale was Bobby Hutton, the barrel of his shotgun at his feet. Next to him was Sherwin Forte, an M1 carbine with a banana clip cradled in his arms. . . ."

The sight blew Eldridge's mind. "Who are these cats?" he thought, recalling the meeting in his later account. "I wondered at them, checking them out carefully. They were so cool and it seemed to me not unconscious of the electrifying effect they were having on everybody in the room."

Everyone had maintained that reverent absolute silence as the Panthers lined themselves in the chairs along the wall. The stillness was broken when one of the coalition group asked if the Panthers wanted to make a speech at the upcoming memorial. Bobby Seale said yes. He was asked what the Panthers wanted to speak about. The program called for four subjects: politics, economics, self-defense and black culture.

" 'It doesn't matter what section we speak under,' Huey said. 'Our message is one and the same. We're going to talk about black people arming themselves in the political arena to see to it that their desires and needs are met. Otherwise there will be a political consequence. And the only culture worth talking about is a revolutionary culture. So it doesn't matter what heading you put on it, we're going to talk about political power growing out of the barrel of a gun.' "

* * * *

Events in Eldridge's life began to accelerate at a dizzying pace from that night on. Within the next twenty-one months Eldridge was to gain his incredible notoriety and fearsome reputation that was to bring those FBI agents and the horde of reporters and TV cameramen to Kennedy Airport in 1975 and keep the world still in awe—and critical appraisal—of him even up to now in 1977.

February would see an even more incredible exhibition of Black Panther awesomeness only days after this first meeting, a conversation between Eldridge and Huey, and Eldridge's joining the party as its minister of information. First, though, let me sketch out a brief Black Panther history up to February, 1967, for those who know it in name only.

The key founders are Huey Newton and Bobby Seale.

Newton was born on February 17, 1942, in Oak Grove, Louisiana, the youngest of seven children. He was named, ironically, after Huey Long, the Louisiana governor who became a veritable dictator in the state and who was assassinated only a few days after Eldridge was born in 1935. His father was a laborer and sometime Baptist preacher. He joined the other thousands of westbound job hunters heading for California in 1944 because of the wartime employment and wound up working at the Oakland naval supply depot. He sent for his family in 1945, and in 1948 joined the Oakland city street department where he was still working when Huey founded the Black Panthers.

Seale was born in Dallas, Texas, October 22, 1936. His father was a carpenter and eventually the Seale family trekked west with all the others.

By the time Newton and Seale met on the Merritt College campus both had run the usual gamut of trouble. Newton once said he was suspended from school thirty-eight times for one reason or another. The stories they were taught went against his grain, even in the earliest grades. *Little Black Sambo* insulted him, particularly since blacks were supposed to identify with that, whereas white kids had *Sleeping Beauty*. When he was about seventeen, a high school counselor insulted him even more by asking him what he was going to do when he graduated, get some sort of manual job? Angered, Newton said no, he was going to college. When the counselor laughed and told him he'd never make it, Newton determined even more to make college. He started then by teaching himself to read. He began by listening to Vincent Price's recordings of *Macbeth* and *Hamlet*, reading along as Price dramatized Shakespeare's lines. The first book Newton ever read on his own after this self-improvement program was Plato's *Republic*. His drive would put most of us to shame.

Seale was in trouble all through his youth, from his days in a government housing project in Berkeley to his stint in the air force in the late 1950s. Before he had entered the service he had bought a $600 set of drums and was so slow in making the payments that the store sent a collection agent to the Ellsworth Air Force Base in South Dakota where Seale was stationed. That got a colonel on his neck, which made Seale mad and before it was over, he was arrested for insubordination and squabbling with the officer. As a result, he was court-martialed and given a bad-conduct discharge. Out of the service, but skilled as a sheet-metal mechanic, he went through a series of firings as employers in government-contract industries learned of his bad discharge. Finally he enrolled at Merritt College in Oakland.

Seale met Huey on campus in September, 1962, as he watched Newton one day holding the riveted attention of about 250 other students in a discussion about black people and the blockade against Cuba. The two got involved with campus black cultural groups, became disgusted with them because of their ineffective nonviolent stances and grew increasingly militant.

Seale admired Newton's aggressive oratory and direct confrontation tactics, and after being accused of directing one of the campus cultural groups, the Soul Students Advisory Council, in a radical direction, they "hit the streets" as the Black Panther Party's first two members. Another thing Seale admired about Newton was Newton's agreement with Malcolm X's view of armed self-defense against the racist power structure in the country and Newton's detailed study of all the federal and state statutes, from the second amendment of the Constitution (giving people the right to bear arms) on down. One of Newton's well-publicized characteristics was that he carried a law book with him as well as a shotgun.

When they got down to black tacks (brass was too

Establishment) about party organization in October, 1966, both Newton and Seale had community-program jobs. Seale worked at the North Oakland Neighborhood Anti-Poverty Center (part of the federal Office of Economic Opportunity, President Johnson's War on Poverty administration agency) teaching a course in Black American History, and Newton was a community organizer. Since the two used a considerable percentage of their incomes from these taxpayer-supported jobs for party organization work, you could say that the American public helped finance the founding of the Black Panther Party.

In October, Seale became chief of the Black Panthers; Newton, the minister of defense; and a mutual much younger friend, Bobby Hutton (Little Bobby), only about sixteen or seventeen, the treasurer.

Their first task was to draw up the Black Panther Party platform and program. It consisted of ten points: (1) We want freedom. We want power to determine the destiny of our black community; (2) We want full employment for our people; (3) We want an end to the robbery of the white man of our black community; (4) We want decent housing, fit for shelter of human beings; (5) We want education for our people that exposes the true nature of this decadent American society. We want education that teaches us our true history and our role in the present-day society; (6) We want all black men to be exempt from military service; (7) We want an immediate end to police brutality and murder of black people; (8) We want freedom for all black men held in federal, state, county and city prisons and jails [meaning release from prison because none had received fair trials]; (9) We want all black people when brought to trial to be tried in court by a jury of their peer group or people from their black communities, as defined by the Constitution of the United States [meaning black jurors]; and (10) We want land, bread, housing, education, clothing, justice and peace. And as our major political objective, a United Nations-supervised plebiscite to be held through the black colony in which only black colonial subjects will be allowed to participate, for the purpose of determining the will of the black people as to their national destiny.

From the language can be seen the influence of all the civil rights movement objectives plus the thinking of Marx, Malcolm X, Mao Tse-tung and Frantz Fanon (famed among radical blacks for his *Wretched of the Earth* which claimed that all "white" systems are inherently evil). The ten-point program sounded quite plausible on the surface, considering the spirit of the times in the mid-1960s. But the real implementer was guns—armed might. Thus the constant show of weapons, the sign of how far the Black Panthers would go.

Once this far, they needed more official position, one that would give them public recognition. So Newton and Seale pooled their taxpayer-funded incomes, got additional help from Hutton and other friends, and rented a small vacant store on 56th and Grove Streets in Oakland for $150 a month. Painting a sign in the window—BLACK PANTHER PARTY FOR SELF-DEFENSE—they opened up shop on January 1, 1967. Three weeks later they had about twenty-five members with classes on gun-handling taught by a reformed drunk who had dropped his booze to pick up the Panther cause.

They now needed regular money to support the party. So they took advantage of the growing popularity of the Red Book, *Quotations from Chairman Mao*, and the radical portion of the University of California student population in Berkeley. Buying gross quantities of the Red Book from the China Book Store in San Francisco for thirty cents a copy and less, they huckstered them at UC for one dollar each and used the profits to finance the party's arsenal, pay rent and other expenses.

That's where things stood when Eldridge Cleaver fell in love at first sight with the Black Panthers that night in February, 1967.

* * * *

With the fourth anniversary of Malcolm X's assassination on February 21, the mass memorial ceremonies were only days away. The Black Panthers were to escort Malcolm's widow from the San Francisco International Airport to the *Ramparts* office in the city where she would meet Eldridge. The jet-garbed armed entourage stunned airport police and shook the *Ramparts* staff as they marched into the magazine's offices. Eldridge allayed fears by telling everybody, "It's all right. It's all right." The Panthers appeared "calm and self-possessed" in contrast to the other chaotic conditions, inside and out, that they had set in motion on their arrival.

The police were on hand, suspiciously asking Warren Hinkle III, *Ramparts'* editor, what was going on and being assured that things were under control. A TV cameraman trying to shoulder his way through the front door was informed he was trespassing. Then he was thrown out, camera and all.

More chaos followed when it came time for Malcolm's widow and the Panthers to leave. Newton sent five men out to clear a path through the thronging spectators to their cars. Watching them leave Eldridge felt his admiration for this group heightening by the second. The TV cameraman who had been thrown out was busy taking pictures. Newton took an envelope from his pocket and held it up in front of the camera lens. When the cameraman shouted and then tried to knock Newton's hand away, Newton turned coolly to one of nearly two dozen police who had gathered and asked him to arrest the man for assault.

Eldridge wrote of it later: "An incredulous look came into the cop's face, then he blurted out: 'If I arrest anybody it'll be you!'

"Huey turned on the cameraman, again placing the envelope in front of the lens. Again the cameraman reached out and knocked Huey's hand away. Huey reached out, snatched the cameraman by the collar and slammed him up against the wall, sending him spinning and staggering down the sidewalk, trying to catch his breath and balance the camera on his shoulder at the same time. . . ."

Moments later, as the Panthers moved towards their cars (again in Eldridge's words), ". . . a big, beefy cop stepped forward. He undid the little strap holding his pistol in his holster and started shouting at Huey, 'Don't point that gun at me! Stop pointing that gun at me!' He kept making gestures as though he was going for his gun.

109

"This was the most tense of moments. Huey stopped in his tracks and stared at the cop."

Ignoring cries from Bobby Seale to leave, "Huey walked to within a few feet of the cop and said, 'What's the matter, you got an itchy finger?'

"The cop made no reply.

" 'You want to draw your gun?' Huey asked him.

"The other cops were calling out for this cop to cool it, to take it easy, but he didn't seem to be able to hear them. He was staring into Huey's eyes, measuring him.

" 'O.K.,' Huey said. 'You big fat racist pig, draw your gun!'

"The cop made no move.

" 'Draw it, you cowardly dog!' Huey pumped a round into the chamber of the shotgun. 'I'm waiting,' he said, and stood there waiting for the cop to draw.

"All the other cops moved back out of the line of fire. I moved back, too," wrote Eldridge, "onto the top step of *Ramparts*. I was thinking, staring at Huey surrounded by all those cops and daring one of them to draw, 'G-----, that nigger is c-r-a-z-y-!'

"Then the cop facing Huey gave it up. He heaved a heavy sigh and lowered his head. Huey literally laughed in his face and then went off up the street at a jaunty pace, disappearing in a blaze of sunlight.

" 'Work out, soul brother!' I was shouting to myself. 'You're the baddest I've ever seen! . . .'"

Eldridge had found an organization to do the work he wanted to do—take on the whole world's Establishment, particularly the American "Oppressor" in the cause of black liberation. The Black Panther Party was just what he needed.

The incident made it into the pages of *Ramparts* and the reading public began to pay attention to the Black Panther Party. Newton was already aware of Eldridge through his writing and the black grapevine, and it was only a short time before he was insisting that Eldridge join the party. There was no question of whether or not he would, except his first realization that perhaps he should continue his efforts to revive Malcolm X's OAAU. Once he decided that cause was a lost one in the greater black one, he yielded and became minister of information, covertly at first, but with parole authorities aware of his actions. At first they did nothing about his Black Panther association, figuring it to be just a small group working within the confines of Oakland. But that view would soon change.

Eldridge's appearance before sixty-five thousand antiwar protestors at Kezar Stadium in San Francisco on April 15, 1967, brought his parole officer and a superior hustling to the *Ramparts* offices. The Kezar rally was the West Coast counterpart of a much larger antiwar demonstration in New York City. Martin Luther King, Jr. spoke in New York and his wife was the featured speaker at the San Francisco gathering. The event was one of the growing protest spectaculars that provided daily front-page headlines. When Eldridge appeared as one of the prominent speakers criticizing America's role in Vietnam, officials became alarmed: he was becoming more than just an angry writer.

Two officials of the California Adult Authority, which amounts to the state's parole board, asked Eldridge to meet them at the *Ramparts* offices a few days after the rally. At the meeting they made it plain that the state was concerned and that his speech had seriously offended members of the Adult Authority. Most important, it had offended Governor Ronald Reagan, who appointed members of the parole board.

The blunt upshot was that if Eldridge continued to speak as he had at Kezar he would not remain out on parole very much longer. What had he said, anyway? Well, a lot of things. He had advocated the Black Panthers' ten-point program. He'd gone much further, calling for self-defense by the blacks and identifying the black struggle with the National Liberation Front's battle in Vietnam. Plainly, in tying in the American civil rights movement with the North Vietnam side, he was supporting our nation's enemies. Any further speeches by Eldridge would have to be approved by his parole officers in advance. When Eldridge argued about his rights, the officers told him flat out that a parolee has no rights. If Governor Reagan didn't like Eldridge's behavior, he could have him tossed back in prison.

They were absolutely correct. In California at that time the Adult Authority was complete dictator over all prisoners. Under the state's indeterminate sentencing law—which has since been repealed—the parole board determined the length of prisoner's sentences within the limits of the penal code, reviewed prisoners and ruled on paroles, and *could even extend* prison terms *beyond* the original sentence, for any wrong behavior while in prison or out on parole. In other words, the California Adult Authority was judge, jury and *the Law*, once a man became convicted of a crime warranting imprisonment in a state penal institution.

Eldridge was as blunt with the two parole officers as

112

they were with him. He said he didn't mind playing all the parolee games, reporting as required four times a month and requesting permission to travel. But he stopped abruptly at having to submit his speeches or any of his writings for approval. He carried his bluntness beyond the *Ramparts* office conversation about the Kezar affair and had his attorneys begin to file briefs on this restriction of civil rights. The parole board backed down on the censorship issue. But their attempt to censor him, and Eldridge's refusal to budge, set the stage for all that was to follow. The scenario was simple, and very clear: Eldridge and the state were hero and villain. (Which was which depended on where you stood.)

Some of the skirmishes in that battle have been resolved in Eldridge's favor, but the main battle still goes on.

The first skirmish came within two weeks of the parole officials' visit to *Ramparts*.

The Black Panthers had been busy, too, since the Malcolm X memorial in February. They had involved themselves deeply in the police shooting of a young black named Denzil Dowell in Richmond, about twenty miles north of Oakland, but in Contra Costa County adjacent to Alameda County. The community felt it was a case of police murder, and the Black Panthers rallied—investigating the scene, confronting police officers (even to Newton's having another armed face-down with a county sheriff's deputy, where each stood a few feet apart jacking and ejecting shells in and out of the chambers of their shotguns), going to the county seat in Martinez to argue the community's case before the district attorney to prosecute the officer

113

suspected of killing young Dowell. Both sides' stories were played big in the papers, to the embarrassment, frustration and growing anger of the police and to the rising indignation of the public.

In the midst of this, Newton spotted another article in the paper to the effect that the state legislature was in the process of considering passage of a gun-control law. With protests of all kinds becoming more radical daily, California, like other states, was growing increasingly fearful of guns in the hands of heated citizens who didn't like the way the government governed. Newton immediately came forth with a plan for the Panthers to go to the capital in Sacramento and make their opposition to any such gun control known. Aware that this was big news and that the press would be well represented he worked out a message to have ready to read to the world.

So, on May 2, 1967, two dozen Panthers, twenty of them armed with shotguns and rifles, parked alongside the state capital building, lined up and marched the few feet to the steps and up into the lobby. Spotted of course before they entered the building, they had already attracted a crowd of stunned onlookers. Inside, there were more people, all gaping. Then newsmen arrived.

Bobby Seale was in charge, the Panthers having voted that Newton stay back in Oakland for fear of getting shot. Seale asked where the assembly—the state's lower house—was meeting. Someone pointed the way and the Panthers followed, holding their guns, with shells in the chambers, pointed skyward or to the ground. Photographers and TV cameramen by now were falling over one another to get pictures. They kept

114

backing up ahead of the advancing, menacing Panthers. There was such confusion that newsmen jostled one guard attempting to halt the oncoming blacks, against the wall, deactivating him; seeing this, another guard, commenting about the Panthers "having the guns," actually opened the door for them.

Once inside the assembly, with reporters and photographers aiding the wild confusion, capital guards managed, with much difficulty, to get Seale and the Panthers back out and down to a smaller room to discuss matters. Here Seale pulled out the Panther statement and read it aloud:

"The Black Panther Party for Self-Defense calls upon the American people to take careful note of the racist California legislature which is now considering legislation aimed at keeping the black people disarmed and powerless at the very same time that racist police agencies throughout the country are intensifying the terror, brutality, murder, and repression of the black people. . . . The Black Panther Party . . . believes that the time has come for black people to arm themselves against this terror before it is too late. . . ."

Throughout the hectic affair Seale kept asking officers if they were under arrest, and repeating they had a right to visit the legislature just like any citizen. In the end, no one was arrested at the capital building, and the Panthers left, their main concern now being food. They were all starved.

The caravan of several cars didn't get far. One of the cars had run out of water and was heating up, so Seale stopped at a gas station a few blocks away from the capital building for a refill. It was there that police in droves converged on the group and arrested them. Eldridge, at the scene covering for *Ramparts*, was among them.

The others were concerned for him, knowing the arrest of a parolee meant his going back to prison. Fortunately, Eldridge had received prior permission from his parole officer to come to Sacramento as a reporter. Later, TV footage showed police that Eldridge was, as he insisted, unarmed, holding only a camera instead of a gun, and was standing with other reporters during the encounter rather than accompanying the Panthers. Reluctantly, the authorities released him.

But in doing so, they slapped a load of new restrictions on him, limiting his travel to within San Francisco only. The Bay Bridge and Oakland were off-limits to him. He was to make no speeches or other public appearances. He was ordered not to say anything critical of the California Department of Corrections or any California politicians.

Eldridge decided to cool it, although his attorneys began to challenge the restrictions in the courts. He figured he could keep active enough concentrating on his writing and Panther organizing and communications activities. The Panthers were thinking of starting their own newspaper, which they later did with Eldridge as editor.

But he had another reason for cooling it. Back around Easter time, Eldridge had spoken at a weekend black students' conference in Tennessee (with permission from his parole officers before the Kezar affair) and had gone through another experience of "love at first sight." This time it was with a slender, lissome

116

twenty-two-year-old civil rights worker once allied with Stokely Carmichael and the SNCC—Kathleen Neal. High-colored and delicately featured, with big expressive eyes and Afro hairdo, she was cultured, well-educated, well-traveled, and as if all that weren't enough, of the same radical mind as Eldridge. He related to Kathleen from moment one.

Kathleen's father, Dr. Earnest Neal, is a distinguished sociologist and professor. For a while he was also a foreign-service officer, a deputy director for the U.S. Agency for International Development (AID) in which capacity he developed a prototype community development program. Kathleen's mother was a social activist whose interests Kathleen shared—and intensified.

Kathleen grew up near college campuses and in international settlements and thus early became exposed to international power politics. By the time she was sixteen she had traveled around the world, and had lived in such far-flung places as New Delhi, Liberia, Sierra Leone and the Philippines. An honor student at schools in these nations, she went on to higher education at home, attending the George School in Pennsylvania, and Oberlin College.

The "model daughter" image changed radically in college. Gene Marine, in his excellent book, *The Black Panthers*, says Kathleen also attended Barnard for a semester after leaving Oberlin during the period that her views were rapidly altering because of her growing interest in the civil rights movement. Marine quotes her as saying, "I was learning things [at Barnard] that I was not learning in school. I began to get educated in the true sense. I began to relearn things about the system, and I developed a new ideological perspective. It's not an American perspective—it's a black perspective. It's a matter of not being brainwashed any more."

She left school and went to work with the New York chapter of SNCC. Later she went to Atlanta as SNCC's campus program secretary, and it was in this capacity that she organized the Easter students' conference in Nashville at which Eldridge spoke. Her father took a dim view of her civil rights work and after she joined SNCC he would have nothing to do with her. When Eldridge entered the picture, Dr. Neal's views of his daughter dimmed even more.

In an interview with Bob Hayes of the *San Francisco Examiner* in June, 1976, Kathleen recalled her first meeting with Eldridge that Easter weekend in Tennessee. "Eldridge says it was love at first sight, but I was sort of frightened. Eldridge had just gotten out of jail, and he still had what we call a 'prisoner's mask,' a face without smiles."

But she was attracted, she told the *Examiner*. "It was the way Eldridge expressed himself, and the seriousness of his writing, but mostly, it was the fact that I gained something from his experiences. Here was a man who had been discarded, to be forgotten, but had resurrected himself and become more dynamic.

"I felt that if a man could survive what he had, he must have been an extremely unusual man of great strength; not someone easily bought off or broken, someone you could have confidence in."

The question of whether she would have been just as content marrying a successful academician or businessman, the *Examiner*'s Hayes wrote, "brought

Kathleen almost to tears of laughter."

She gasped, "My God, what would we have talked about? I was completely absorbed with the movement. That's all I wanted to talk about. Clothes and cars meant nothing to me. I was only interested in social and political change."

There was only one thing for her to do, as far as Eldridge was concerned. Kathleen must come to the Bay Area right away and join in the Black Panther movement. She heeded his urging and moved to California shortly after the students' conference and became a Black Panther communications secretary.

* * * *

So Eldridge didn't want to jeopardize this "good thing" he had going and decided to play along with the parole authorities. In time the travel restriction to Oakland was lifted so that he was able to cover *Ramparts* assignments—as long as the authorities approved them first. Everything went along fairly easily until October.

About 5:00 A.M., October 28, 1967, Oakland Patrolman John Frey radioed police headquarters that he had a Panther car in sight that he was going to stop for a check. Huey Newton was in the car. Exactly what took place was debated in court for months later on, but the bottom line that morning was that Officer Frey was shot and killed and Newton was charged with his murder.

Up to now, the name Eldridge Cleaver was familiar only to the Bay Area and California public. No longer. It is at this point in Eldridge's life that he became a national figure.

Newton's arrest deprived the Black Panthers of leadership. Bobby Seale was still in jail because of the Sacramento affair. The only person with any leadership or speaking ability was Eldridge, the minister of information. He became acting chief of the Black Panther Party. The next thirteen months—almost to the day, November 27, 1968, when the events of the times forced him to become a fugitive—would also make him a foremost target for all forces trying to keep Black Power from getting out of control. Or, as the Establishment viewed the threat—to keep Black Power from *gaining* control.

CHAPTER FOUR

TARGET

Most urgent and immediate of the problems facing the Panthers was of course to aid Huey Newton. He had been wounded in the shoot-out with Frey and was now in the hospital at San Quentin (for "safekeeping" was the official reason) with the four bullet holes in his abdomen. To a man, Panther members called the whole thing a frame; and they had considerable support from many parts of the community, too.

For Eldridge, the "rescue" of Huey posed serious problems. He'd carefully remained semiactive because of the parole restrictions imposed after the Sacramento affair in May. Some of the restrictions—primarily travel limitations—had been lifted. But he was under scrutiny by top officials. Even though his parole officer and the officer's supervisor who had talked with him at the *Ramparts* offices considered him a "model parolee," higher Adult Authority officials didn't like him. The two parole officers had told him those higher authorities were ready to revoke his parole at the first excuse.

121

So at the outset of the "Free Huey!" campaign, which would eventually reach to many parts of the nation—campaign buttons and posters appeared in New York and elsewhere—Eldridge knew that any action he took in Newton's behalf would risk his own return to prison. He willingly took the chance. Huey was his hero, too, and leader in the most important cause in the world, liberation of the black people. Eldridge's decision was widely quoted as almost a kind of rallying cry: "Helping Huey stay out of the gas chamber is more important than my staying out of San Quentin."

He went for broke, using all the media—TV, newspapers, magazines, posters, leaflets, the "Free Huey!" buttons. Realizing he was living on borrowed time, Eldridge publicly declared he wanted to get as much done as he could before time ran out.

The Newton-Frey shooting, and thus the increased Panther activity, came at the worst possible time. The nation had just gone through another long, hot summer of widespread riots. There was increasing antidraft protest, in which Oakland figured prominently. Barely a week before Newton and Frey had that fatal meeting, the Oakland Induction Center had been one of the targets in the Stop-The-Draft-Week campaign which culminated in the famed March on the Pentagon. Starting on Monday, October 16, hundreds of protesters thronged the Oakland Induction Center, jamming into the doorway in the attempt to close it down. The nationwide campaign had received wide advance publicity so Oakland police were out in force. Many demonstrators were arrested the first day. On Tuesday, the 17th, over four thousand protesters showed up. The confrontation increased toughness on both sides. On Friday, October 20th, according to some reports, ten thousand demonstrators converged on the draft center. More hundreds were arrested and many pummeled, bruised and beaten as wedge formations of Oakland police, reinforced by sheriff's deputies and highway patrolmen, battled the crowds back. Reporters described it as the worst example of police activity they had ever witnessed. The *San Francisco Chronicle* sued, and successfully, enjoining Oakland police from ever repeating such uncalled-for brutality.

There were two sides to the matter. As a police reporter for the *Herald & News* out in the Livermore-Pleasanton area where the sheriff's department Santa Rita Rehabilitation Center was located (where many of the arrestees were brought), I talked to many sheriff's deputies called to extra duty at the Oakland Induction Center affair. They told me that orders to "cool it" and just hold crowds back became almost impossible when ragged, unkempt youths came up and spit in their faces or threw human feces at them. So the blame was not all on the Oakland police. Provocation and brutality came from both sides.

But sympathies were leaning more and more toward the demonstrators. Police literally were "pigs." That reputation made officers even more uptight, trigger-happy, and, yes, vengeful. It was the old story: force begets force, hate begets hate.

Oakland police, especially, considered it all "civil war." The Panthers had been more and more aggressive, ever since the Denzil Dowell affair in Richmond and Sacramento. They made it a regular habit to "patrol" the police patrol cars. The weekly

Panther paper stridently cried brutality in all of its stories, polarizing matters between oppressors and "the oppressed people of the world."

As the new leader in this war, Eldridge became the most natural of targets. When the campaign for Newton attracted support from the Peace and Freedom Party (PFP) in late November and December, matters intensified even more. The PFP was an all-white organization created primarily in opposition to the draft. But it argued that it was interested in all political affairs, and since Newton's was clearly a political affair, they supported the campaign. The Black Panthers and the PFP joined forces, with Panther members diving into a mass petition-signing campaign to get the PFP on next year's presidential ballot. They succeeded. Eldridge figured prominently in bringing the Panther-PFP alliance about. So he became an even greater threat to the Establishment—and thus, a bigger target.

December was also a significant month for Eldridge. He and Kathleen were married.

They were still honeymooners in their San Francisco apartment when at 3:00 A.M. on January 15, 1968, while the Cleavers were socializing with artist Emory Douglas, whose poster work for the Panthers had been attracting much attention, members of the special tactical squad of the San Francisco Police Department pounded on their door, demanding entry. When Eldridge refused, they kicked the door down. The police held everyone at gunpoint while they stormed through the rooms. They wouldn't say exactly what they were searching for, obviously anything incriminating. Most obviously guns, because if they had found those in Eldridge's possession—as a parolee—they would have had the perfect reason to send him packing back to prison. They uncovered nothing and stalked out.

Similar raids were held on other Panther members. One on Bobby Seale's uncovered some guns and put him under arrest again; he had been released on December 8, 1967, from the Sacramento affair, and now was in custody once more, this time on what many considered a totally trumped-up charge: conspiracy to commit murder.

The campaign to free Newton developed into a massive affair at the Oakland Auditorium February 17, 1968, coincident with Huey's twenty-sixth birthday. The huge rally featured Stokely Carmichael in his first appearance following his well-publicized tour of revolutionary countries, James Forman, and H. Rap Brown, a new leader, after Carmichael, of SNCC.

Over five thousand people showed up, and since the auditorium building is only a few hundred yards from the Alameda County Courthouse where Newton would eventually be tried, the rally was a distinct fist-shaking in the face of authorities. And of course, the raised clenched fist was by then the physical emblem of the "revolution to liberate the oppressed black people of the world."

The February 17th rally became more than just a localized "Free Huey!" campaign forum. The earlier alliance of the Black Panthers and the Peace and Freedom Party, while an eyebrow-raiser in the Bay Area, had held nothing of great importance—yet—for the nations at large. White America, particularly, paid it little heed. But the mass rally at the Oakland

Auditorium also became the stage from which the Panthers announced their alliance with SNCC—and this did rattle cages all across the country. SNCC was all black. The PFP was all white. SNCC had long been measured as a powerful force in the radicalizing civil rights movement. The Panther-SNCC alliance added much weight to the earlier affiliation with the PFP. The authorities' anxiety heightened considerably.

Eleven days after the Oakland rally, McGraw-Hill published Eldridge's *Soul on Ice*. This immediately focused more national attention on Eldridge, and in the Bay Area made him an even more notorious figure. Now he had become a national—and soon, worldwide—spokesman for the black liberation cause. And because of his ruthless directness and the caustic, accusatory "street language" with which he had written, he was the prime target of local police and state politicians. That such a band as the Panthers would have a "firebrand voice" as eloquent as Cleaver's was the ultimate threat against the Establishment.

Tension tightened even more when at the official founding convention of the California Peace and Freedom Party in Richmond on March 16, 1968, Cleaver became the party's candidate for the president of the United States. This made even the most uninterested sit up. It was mockery, a sick joke, impudence and a threat to the pigs and politicians. That such a man as Eldridge Cleaver might in the wildest stretch of the imagination sit in the Oval Office of the White House one day boggled any mind —except, of course, the growing numbers of citizens who supported the black cause. It was a futile effort, to be sure. For one thing, Eldridge was only thirty-three, and thus ineligible to hold the presidency under the Constitution's thirty-five-year-old age limit. That he campaigned and many campaigned for him, in blatant disregard of that Constitutional stipulation, made the whole affair that much more of a mockery and sham.

At the March 16th PFP convention, Eldridge made further statements which added to his stature as a target. "What we need," he declared, "is a revolution in the white mother country and national liberation for the black colony."

This talk about the "white mother country" and "black colony" was common in revolutionary thinking at that point in time, and Eldridge had written much about the two distinct sets of "political dynamics" at work in the country. The language shows how far many considered the black-white polarization in the country had gone, and how hardened they had become. The "white mother country" was being shaken at its foundations, and the "black colony" within it was intent on liberating itself after centuries of being held down.

Eldridge's reasoning was always persuasive; it always set him apart from the wild-eyed revolutionary. At the convention he chided the press and urged it not to refer to the black revolution as consisting merely of "anarchists who want to wreck the system," or as "militant antiwhite violent black extremists." To do so was to misunderstand the truth, to overlook so many of the factors making up the whole picture. There *was* at the time a distinct oppressor-oppressed quality, evident in all the events, that was becoming clearer every day. Black people, he said, were resentful because "they recognized that what they wanted to happen was not happening and that a lot of their activity was being

127

distorted by the white people who had another primary interest."

The Panthers' alliances with the PFP and SNCC were moves to broaden that view and to simplify the great social-cultural issue in such plain and simple terms. All other rhetoric simply confused that simple issue.

There *was* much truth in all that Eldridge said. Not enough people would admit it, so matters deteriorated to where the blacks' *methods* for achieving their ends hardened into such a physical determination that white America couldn't tolerate it.

Historian William O'Neill observed the whole development accurately when commenting about the status of events as they existed in 1969, after another year of this white-black, "mother country-black colony" revolution: "The Black Panther experience was doubly tragic: first, because they were blind to the fact that you can't make a revolution in a country where most people support the government; second, because the government couldn't see that either, and persisted in treating a head cold as an epidemic" (*Coming Apart*, p. 189).

With the vested interest the nation's press has in "being where the action is," and considering that action in those days centered on violence and revolutionary behavior, Eldridge's comments and Panther political activities with the PFP and SNCC were made to appear as an epidemic. The local press made it into a veritable plague. All of which outlined Eldridge even more sharply as the target to hit.

With the insanity that was to break out across the

nation within two weeks of Eldridge's March 16th speech not even the most perceptive social diagnostician suspected the obvious epidemic was only a head cold.

On April 3, the Black Panthers were startled at the sudden interruption of their regular meeting at St. Augustine's Catholic Church on 27th and West Streets in Oakland. The doors were shoved open by a phalanx of police officers with shotguns accompanied by a white monsignor and a black preacher. What they were hunting for they never said—but it was suspected (and still is) that they were hoping to find Eldridge and / or Bobby Seale. Seale was in Los Angeles, and Eldridge had left only moments before, after receiving an "urgent" phone call. St. Augustine's priest, Father Neil, who up to that time never really believed all he heard about police harassment of the Panthers, was outraged at what he saw. He called a press conference for the next day, April 4th, at which he denounced the Oakland Police Department. But his conference was submerged under the greater tragedy of Dr. Martin Luther King's assassination in Memphis.

Dr. King's murder chilled people's hearts. What—*what*—was happening to America? His death brought a round of new rioting across the nation. Some occurred throughout the Bay Area, but it was far worse elsewhere. What the public probably still does not realize is that the Panthers played a good part in quelling potential riots in numerous Bay Area communities before they occurred. More than one writer of Panther history notes that members were constantly on the run from one trouble spot to another in San Francisco and Oakland and adjoining cities

129

telling anguished outraged blacks not to take out their revenge for Dr. King's death by new upheavals of their own. The Panthers had the best of reasons for doing this—aside from any peacemaker characteristic: They were painfully aware that they were targets of the police and that black outbreaks would very easily be charged to them. They wanted nothing to happen to bring more trouble on their own heads.

The Panthers were in police sights enough already, specifically during the past few days as they had been preparing for the Black Community Barbecue Picnic planned for April 7th at deFremery Park. They had been advertising the picnic heavily, even going around the West Oakland section and other areas in a sound truck inviting people. The police had opposed the affair from the start in a variety of moves, at first trying to stop the use of the park and later getting the city to impose all sorts of regulations on behavior, such as no speeches, no sound equipment, no passing out of campaign literature.

The purpose of the picnic was twofold. It was a fund-raiser both for the Newton defense fund and the Black Panther Party Campaign Fund. By this time, in addition to Eldridge's PFP candidacy for the U.S. presidency, the Panthers were running three candidates of their own: Huey P. Newton for Congress in the 7th congressional district; Bobby Seale for the 17th assembly district seat in Alameda County; and Kathleen Cleaver for the 18th assembly district seat in San Francisco.

The Panthers didn't want to jeopardize anything they were doing, so they did their best to curb unrest in the aftermath of the King assassination. Still, his murder set up new tensions everywhere. Something had to break some place.

It did, two days later, the night of April 6, 1968.

On the afternoon of Saturday, April 6, 1968, Eldridge was in the *Ramparts* office in San Francisco dictating the words of "Requiem for Nonviolence,"—a piece requested by the editor on what the assassination of Martin Luther King, Jr. meant for the future.

". . . It is hard to put words on this tape because words are no longer relevant. Action is all that counts now. And maybe America is incapable of understanding *anything* relevant to human rights. I think that America has already committed suicide and we who now thrash within its dead body are also dead in part and parcel of the corpse. America is truly a disgusting burden upon this planet. A burden upon all humanity. And if we here in America. . . ."

The phone rang. Eldridge answered it and hurried out. "Requiem" was never finished. The next morning his editor and Kathleen knew why.

The Sunday *Oakland Tribune* gave the reason on its front page, just to the left of a photo of Mrs. King and Rev. Ralph Abernathy bearing the caption: "Mrs. King Discusses Her Husband's Work and Its Meaning." The *Tribune's* story about Eldridge came under a three-deck headline:"ONE KILLED, 4 SHOT IN GUN BATTLE HERE."

"One suspect was killed," the story below read, "two wounded and two Oakland police officers were shot and wounded Saturday night during a 90-minute gun battle and seige in West Oakland.

"The slain suspect, shot as he emerged from a barricaded house at 1218 28th St., was tentatively identified by police as Bobby Hutton, about 18, a member of the Black Panthers.

"Another Black Panther member, minister of information Eldridge Cleaver, was wounded in the lower left leg. The other wounded man. . . ."

Kathleen recalls that she woke up that Sunday morning to find that Eldridge "was back in prison. When I went to see him all shot up, sitting in a wheelchair with half his hair burned out, I realized that he would be going back to prison and he might never come out again."

The details of exactly what happened during those ninety minutes shortly after 9:00 P.M., April 6, 1968, have never been satisfactorily resolved.

For his part in that night's affair, Eldridge is charged with three counts of attempted murder and three counts of assault with a deadly weapon on a police officer. The combined penalties for the crimes with which Eldridge is charged total some seventy-five years.

The truth of what happened that night exists in many different versions in the memories of those involved, in the grand jury record, in the police reports, and in Eldridge's affidavit written two weeks later, on April 19, 1968. I believe in letting accounts speak for themselves, so to continue the *Tribune's* Sunday coverage (condensed only to eliminate some needless names and repetitions):

". . . Hutton, who pleaded guilty last year to a misdemeanor charge of disturbing the state legislature during a Panther visit to Sacramento was killed instantly during the West Oakland gun battle.

"Neither officer was wounded critically. Two other officers were treated for minor injuries.

"Deputy Police Chief Robert R. Cazadd said the gun battle grew out of a definite attempt to ambush police.

"Police said the shooting began after a patrol car stopped to question the occupants of three parked cars in the 2900 block of Union St.

"When police officer Richard R. Jensen stepped from the passenger's side of the cruiser, police said, he was shot without warning.

"As his patrol partner, Nolan R. Darnell, stepped from the car he was grazed with buckshot.

"Most of the occupants of the cars fled, several around the corner into a house at 1218 28th Street.

"Police arrested four persons believed to have been in the parked cars and laid siege in the house where the others were barricaded.

"Police and firemen quickly sealed off the two-block area and police officers, crouched behind cars, traded shots with the men inside the building. Floodlights gave the scene the appearance of a movie set. . . .

"Some 20 minutes later, after police gunfire had broken a front window and tear gas had been fired into the front room, the men inside called out that they wanted to surrender.

". . . The men began to emerge, one at a time, from the building. As the first came out, there was a cry that he had a gun, several shots were fired and the man collapsed and fell to the sidewalk dead.

"The other two men, their hands above their heads, came out of the building and surrendered. . . ."

A follow-up story appeared in the April 8 *Tribune*:

". . . All the suspects are Negroes. Police said all are members of the Black Panther Party.

"Police seized an arsenal of weapons and ammunition. Some of the 18 rifles and handguns were of military type and are not obtainable on the open market.

"Hutton, the dead youth . . . was hit at least seven times. Police said that Hutton and Cleaver were holed up at 1218 28th St. and were armed with two 9mm automatic rifles and a large supply of ammunition, some of it armor piercing. . . .

"Deputy Police Chief Robert Cazadd said that one of the suspects (it turned out to be Hutton) wearing a coat left the house and ran towards the officers. He said that Hutton was crouched over and the officers could not see his hands.

"Officers called for him to halt, said Cazadd, and when he didn't, they opened fire. . . ."

Deputy Police Chief Cazadd's version in this story of how the gunfight started was that it was a "planned ambush" and began "about 9:07 P.M. . . ." when the two officers Jensen and Darnell stopped their patrol car to "check a man they said was crouching down behind an auto with Florida license plates. . . ."

Police said when they were getting out of their cars ". . . they were caught in a cross fire from both sides of the street and in the rear. Their car was blasted with 49 bullet holes. Another police car was burned. . . ."

Further description of the siege of the 28th Street house added, ". . . officers fired barrages of tear gas into the building. One canister started a fire but it was quickly extinguished. . . .

"Black Panther Party Chairman Bobby Seale was

134

bitterly critical of the police action. He told a press conference . . . that witnesses told him that Hutton was shot while attempting to surrender. . . ."

That's the substance of the night's events. Eight Panthers, including Eldridge, were arrested. The *Tribune's* accounts at least set up a general framework in which all the varying accounts will eventually be matched, disputed, or denied. The main questions in dispute, of course, are: who shot first, police or Panthers? What, really, was Eldridge's part in the night's affair? How was Bobby Hutton really killed—by "brutal pigs" when he surrendered, or by uptight officers when he was "escaping?"

There are numerous accounts. Gene Marine in *The Black Panthers*, put together many of them in nearly forty pages, from depositions by many of those involved; interviews by himself, other *Ramparts* colleagues and reporters for other media who interviewed eyewitnesses; and from the most official record thus far aside from police reports—the grand jury proceedings.

In summary, he points out, "The same grand jury that indicted the Panthers [on varying charges of assault, attempted murder and intent to kill] for the occurrences of that night took another action, also; they found the police killing of Bobby James Hutton, age seventeen, entirely justified. The Black Panthers are equally certain: 'The pigs murdered li'l Bobby. . . .'

"So much emotion surrounds the event, so many words have been uttered or written, that it comes as something of a shock for a reporter to realize that neither can be right, in the sense that neither can *know*. The grand jury heard only police witnesses and statements from some of the arrested Panthers which were later retracted as having been extracted under duress [the grand jury was not told that the statements had been repudiated, although affidavits to that effect had already been filed in a Federal court]. They never heard any Panther's side of the story. . . ."

One eyewitness account has received wide publication: Eldridge's. It appears in *Post-Prison Writings*, a selection of *Ramparts* article reprints. It is so vivid, it is worth excerpting at length:

"I think that the so-called shoot-out on 28th Street was the direct result of frantic attempts by the Oakland Police Department to sabotage the Black Community Barbecue Picnic, which the Black Panther Party had set up for April 7th in deFremery Park. The shoot-out occurred the night before the scheduled picnic. . . .

"It is a rule of our party that no well-known member of the party is to be out on the Oakland streets at night unless accompanied by two or more other people, because we felt that if the Oakland cops ever caught one of us alone like that there was a chance that such a one might be killed and there would be only racist pig cops for witnesses: Verdict of the Coroner's Inquest, 'Justifiable Homicide.' Period. After the way they tried to murder our leader, Minister of Defense Huey P. Newton, we were not taking any chances. So on the night of April 6, the car I was driving was being followed by two carloads of Panthers and I was on my way to David Hilliard's house at 34th and Magnolia. In the car with me were David Hilliard, Wendell Wade, and John Scott, all members of the Black Panther Party.

"We were only a few blocks away from David's house

when, all of a sudden, I was overcome by an irresistible urge, a necessity, to urinate, and so I turned off the brightly lighted street we were on (I think it was 30th Street, but I'm not sure, not being overly familiar with the area), pulled to the curb, stopped the car, got out and started relieving myself. The two Panther cars following us pulled up behind to wait. While I was in the middle of this call of nature, a car came around the corner from the direction that we ourselves had come, and I found myself in danger of being embarrassed, I thought, by a passing car. So I cut off the flow, then, and awkwardly hurried around to the other side of the car, to the sidewalk, to finish what had already been started and what was most difficult to stop—I recall that I did soil my trousers somewhat. But this car, instead of passing, stopped, and a spotlight from it was turned on and beamed my way. I could see it was the cops, two of them. They got out of the car and stood there, not leaving the car, each standing just outside. One of them shouted, 'Hey you, walk out into the middle of the street with your hands up, quick!'

"For the second time, I had to deal with a ticklish situation and I was so close to the end that I could not resist finishing. I shouted back to the cops, 'O.K., O.K.!' I turned, trying to zip up my fly and get out into the middle of the street. Common sense told me that I'd best have my hands up by the time I cleared the front of my car. But before I cleared, the cop on the passenger side of his car started shouting and firing his gun, and then the other cop started shooting. I am not sure they were shooting at me because the lights from their car were shining brightly at me, blocking my vision. But the explosions from their guns sounded right in my face

137

and so, startled, I dove for cover in front of my car. The Panthers in the other two cars started yelling at the cops and honking their horns and getting out of their cars, and the brothers who were in my car scrambled out of the passenger side.

"Above my head, the windshield of my car shattered and I looked behind me. There was another cop car at the other end of the street, from which shots were also being fired at us. In fact, shots seemed to be coming from everywhere; it sounded like the entire block had erupted with gunfire. It took only a split second to see that they had us in a cross fire, so I shouted to the brothers, 'Scatter! Let's get out of here!' Our best bet, it was clear, was to make it across the street and that's where we headed. As we started across, one of the Panthers, Warren Wells, got hit and let out an agonized yelp of pain as he fell to the ground. I dove for the pavement, in about the middle of the street, with bullets ricocheting off the pavement all around me and whizzing past my head. I was being fired at from several different directions and for the second time within the space of a few minutes I could taste death on my tongue. But I kept crawling across the street as fast as I could and I truthfully didn't know whether I had been hit or not, whether I was dead or dying. I was hurting all over from scraping against the pavement and I was still being shot at. I saw a couple of Panthers run between two houses and got to my feet and followed them. A cop with a shotgun was running after me, shooting. I didn't have a gun but I wished that I had! (O, how I wish that I had!!!)

"As I ran between those two houses, I saw a Panther climbing over what looked like a fence. I hit it just as soon as he was over, only to find out, as I climbed up, that it was some sort of a shed and I was on top of it and the cop behind me was still shooting at me with the shotgun. I dove off and onto the ground on the other side, landing on top of Bobby Hutton. Before I had recovered from the jolt of my leap, I was wishing that I had never come over the top of that shed, that I had stayed there to face that cop with that blazing shotgun, because Little Bobby and I were boxed in. The shed at our backs spanned the space between the houses on either side of us, and although the area in front of us was clear all the way out to the street, we could not budge from that little nook because the street was filled with cops and they were pumping shots at us as though shooting was about to go out of style. In the dark, I could not see that Little Bobby had a rifle, until it started to bark, producing a miraculous effect: the cops, cowardly pigs from their flat feet to their heads, all ran for cover. The few seconds that this gave us allowed us to find a door into the basement of the house to our right, and we dove inside. We were just in time to escape a murderous fusillade of shots that scoured the tiny area we had just abandoned.

"But if jumping over the shed had been like going from the frying pan into the fire, entering that house defies description. The walls were like tissue paper and the pigs were shooting through them from all four sides at once. It was like being the Indians in all the cowboy movies I had ever seen. What saved us for the moment was an eighteen-inch-high cement foundation running around the cellar at the base of the wall. We lay down flat against the floor while the bullets ripped through the walls. This unrelenting fire went on for about half an hour, and then it stopped and the pigs started lobbing in tear gas. While the gas was being pumped in through the windows, Little Bobby and I took the opportunity to fortify the walls with whatever we could lay our hands on: furniture, tin cans, cardboard boxes—it was hopeless but we tried it anyway. While I was standing up trying to move a thick board over against the wall, I was struck in the chest by a tear gas canister fired through a window. It knocked me down and almost out. Little Bobby, weak from the gas, was coughing and choking, but he took all my clothes off in an effort to locate a wound in the dark, patting me down for the moist feel of blood.

"The pigs started shooting again and we had to hit the deck. The material we had stacked along the wall was blown away by what sounded like machine-gun fire. We decided to stay in there and choke to death if necessary rather than walk out into a hail of bullets. Above the din of gunfire, we could hear the voices of people yelling at the cops to stop shooting, calling them murderers and all kinds of names, and this gave us the strength and the hope to hang on. The tear gas was not as hard to endure as I had imagined it to be. My lungs were on fire, nose and eyes burning, but after a while I couldn't feel anything. Once Little Bobby told me he was about to pass out. He did, but he came to before long, and the two of us lay there counting the minutes and ducking the bullets that were too numerous to count. One of the shots found my leg and my foot with an impact so painful and heavy that I was sure I no longer had two legs. But it didn't seem to matter because I was also sure that it was only a matter of seconds before one of the bullets found a more vital spot. In my mind, I was actually saying goodbye to the world and I was sure that Little Bobby was doing the same thing. Lying there pinned down like that, there was nothing else to do. If there was I couldn't think of it. I said goodbye to my wife, and an image of her dancing for me, as I had watched her do so many times before, floated past my mind's eye, and I reached out to touch her, to kiss her goodbye with my fingers. Then my mind seemed to dwell on crowds of people, masses of people, millions of people, as though the whole human race, all the men and women who had ever lived, seemed to present themselves to my view. I saw images of parades, crowd scenes in auditoriums. I remembered the people at the rally in the Oakland Auditorium, the surging, twisting sea of people at the Peace and Freedom Party Convention at the Richmond Auditorium; these two events somehow coupled in my mind. I saw throngs of students at Merritt College, at San Francisco State College, and at U.C. Berkeley, and then I heard Little Bobby ask me, 'What are we going to do?'

"I felt an impotent rage at myself because all I could tell him was to keep his head down, that head with its beautiful black face which I would watch a little later, again powerless, as the mad dogs outside blasted him into eternity. Was it in cold blood? It was in the coldest of blood. It was murder. MURDER! And that must never be forgotten: the Oakland Police Department MURDERED Little Bobby, and they cannot have that as a victory. Every pig on that murderous police force is guilty of murdering Little Bobby; and lying, hypocritical Chief Gains is Murderer No. 1. And we must all swear by Little Bobby's blood that we will not rest until Chief Gains is brought to justice, either in the courts or in the streets; and until the bloodthirsty troops of the Oakland Police Department no longer exist in the role of an occupying army with its boots on the neck of the black community, with its guns aimed at the black community's head, an evil force with its sword of terror thrust into the heart of the black community.

"The rest of the story is madness, pain, and humiliation at the hands of the Pigs. They shot firebombs into the cellar, turning it into a raging inferno, and we could not stand the heat, could not breathe the hot air with lungs already raw from the tear gas. We had to get out of there, to flee from certain death to face whatever awaited us outside. I called out to the Pigs and told them that we were coming out. They said to throw out the guns; I was lying beneath a window, so Little Bobby passed me the rifle and I threw it outside, still lying on my back. Then Little Bobby helped me to my feet and we tumbled through the door. There were pigs in the windows above us in the house next door, with guns pointed at us. They told us not to move, to raise our hands. This we did, and an army of pigs ran up from the street. They started kicking and cursing us, but we were already beyond any pain, beyond feeling. The pigs told us to stand up. Little Bobby helped me to my feet. The pigs pointed to a squad car parked in the middle of the street and told us to run to it. I told them that I couldn't run. Then they snatched Little Bobby away from me and shoved him forward, telling him to run to the car. It was a sickening sight. Little Bobby, coughing and choking on the night air that was burning his lungs as my own were burning from the tear gas, stumbled forward as best he could, and after he had traveled about ten yards the Pigs cut loose on him with their guns, and then they turned to me. But before they could get into anything, the black people in the neighborhood who had been drawn to the site by the gunfire and commotion began yelling at them, calling the pigs murderers, telling them to leave me alone. And a face I will never forget, the face of the captain with the murder blue eyes, loomed up.

" 'Where are you wounded?' he asked me.

"I pointed out my wound to him. The Pig of Pigs looked down at my wound, raised his foot and stomped on the wound.

" 'Get him out of here,' he told the other pigs, and they took me away.

"Why am I alive? While at Highland Hospital, a pig said to me: 'You ain't going to be at no barbecue picnic tomorrow. You the barbecue now!' Why did Little Bobby die? It was not a miracle, it just happened that way. I know my duty. Having been spared my life, I don't want it. I give it back to our struggle. Eldridge Cleaver died in that house on 28th Street, with Little Bobby, and what's left is force: fuel for the fire that will rage across the face of this racist country and either purge it of its evil or turn it into ashes. I say this for Little Bobby, for Eldridge Cleaver who died that night, for every black man, woman, and child who ever died here in Babylon, and I say it to racist America, that if every voice of dissent is silenced by your guns, by your courts, by your gas chambers, by your money, you will know, that as long as the ghost of Eldridge Cleaver is afoot, you have an ENEMY in your midst. April 19, 1968."

I could make a lot of comments about all of Eldridge's

imagery, his dedication, his resorting once more to biblical terms (the first hint of soul matters for a long time; he had left such matters behind, or maybe better, suppressed beneath his intense activity. They would all surface once again later, when the heat was off). But more important right now is one other account dealing with the night of April 6th. It is in a remarkable news article from the *San Francisco Examiner*, dated April 18, 1971, three years and twelve days later, written by Dexter Waugh. I stumbled across it in yellowing clip files at the Berkeley Public Library:

"Three years after the fatal shooting of Black Panther Party Treasurer Bobby Hutton by Oakland police, a new version of what happened the night of April 6, 1968, has come to light.

"Gwynne Peirson, a black Oakland police officer present during the Panther-police shootout, now says Hutton was killed not because he broke and ran but because police 'got out of control.'

"The incident, which occurred the weekend of Martin Luther King's assassination, was a turning point in Black Panther Party affairs. It led to the flight to Algiers by the Party's prominent minister of information, Eldridge Cleaver, who faced charges of parole violation and other charges arising from the fight.

"The Alameda County Grand Jury, which ruled the police action lawful, heard five police witnesses who said the 17-year-old Hutton was shot while trying to escape.

"Peirson was not asked to testify.

"Other versions by police witnesses were hinted at the time but never surfaced. Civilian witnesses, including reporters, were not allowed near the area during the battle and its immediate aftermath, and consequently the circumstances of Hutton's death remain something of a mystery.

"Court cases presented against six of the eight Panthers arrested that night have focused on the assault on two police officers which set off the chain of events that ended in Hutton's killing. The manner of Hutton's death was ruled immaterial to these proceedings. Peirson was never called by defense or prosecution.

"Peirson, 49, quit the Oakland force last year after 22 years of service. He has written about the incident three years later in his criminology master's thesis for the University of California.

"He said officers started 'shoving' Eldridge Cleaver and Hutton as they surrendered and emerged from the basement of a house on 28th Street in West Oakland, where they had taken refuge after the shooting of two Oakland officers.

"Peirson told the *Examiner* that the police were all worked up for various reasons. They were getting ready to do almost anything.'

"In his thesis, he wrote that 'because of the physical contact between Hutton and the officers, and also because Hutton was walking with his hands in the air at the time, he stumbled while walking and brought his hands down. When his hands came down there was a series of six to nine shots and Bobby Hutton was killed.'

"Peirson, in an interview, said he didn't 'think it was murder. It's just that the thing was completely out of control. They had been firing for half an hour, never knowing where you are shooting—at least I didn't see anything to shoot at. In the end, they didn't have any control over what happened.'

"Peirson said he was standing across the street from the house, behind a telephone pole. Near him an Emeryville policeman who had come to help was kneeling behind a car, pumping off rounds from a 12-gauge shotgun.

" 'He shot up a whole box of shotgun shells, and I don't know what he was shooting at. But he shot up the box and when he was finished he got up and left.'

"Peirson's testimony differs from testimony given to the Grand Jury two weeks after the shooting by five other police officers, three of whom said they shot at Hutton.

"The officers, who were standing closer to Hutton than Peirson was, told the Grand Jury basically the same story.

"They said Cleaver and Hutton emerged from the basement and, accompanied by several officers who had gone down a walkway beside the house to get to them, came to the front of the house.

"Their testimony indicated one or more of the group—suspects and officers—fell to the ground. Reports differed. But the testifying officers agreed they saw Hutton come up in a 'running position.'

"Hutton got about eight or ten steps away, running in a crouched position, according to one officer. The officers said they heard other policemen yelling 'Look out! He's running.'

"One testifying officer hearing the shouts, turned around and fired two rounds from his service revolver at Hutton, who was 'approximately five feet from me . . . running westbound on the sidewalk.'

"Another said he had his " 'carbine slung over my

146

shoulder and I just brought it right around, and I was still in sort of a crouched position, and I fired. Three (times).'

"Peirson received a disability retirement from the Oakland force last year. He said he had passed the promotional exam for sergeant more than once. Although placed on the eligibility list, he was not promoted while others were.

"He now works as a lecturer and training director at the University of Missouri's criminology department in St, Louis.

"Peirson wrote in his thesis that he stated to a team of police and district attorney's investigators that Hutton did not make any attempt to escape before being shot.

" 'Approximately a month later selected statements were submitted to the Grand Jury. In addition, several officers were called to testify before that jury. As a result of the statements and the testimony . . . the jury found that Bobby Hutton was killed while trying to escape and that therefore his death was "justifiable homicide".'

"Peirson wrote that he was not called to testify, that his statement was not seen by the Grand Jury, and that in fact his statement, taken down by a stenographer, was never transcribed from shorthand.

"Alameda County District Attorney Lowell Jensen said he could not make any comment as to why Pierson's views were excluded.

"Peirson told the *Examiner* that when his opinion became known to other officers, 'pressure' was exerted against him.

"Peirson was born and raised in Oakland. He has two

sons, aged 12 and 22. He joined the Oakland force in 1947 as a patrolman.

"He worked 11 years in the patrol division and 11 years as a homicide investigator."

* * * *

Clearly, the night of April 6, 1968, eclipses anything that had occurred in Eldridge's life up to that point. Even his "insurrectionary act" days didn't contain such harrowing events, although they certainly marked his soul and led him to an important landmark: what it meant to go astray. Isn't that what he had written so long ago back in that exquisitely private cell on the honor block?

And now, this Saturday night in 1968—by now midnight or after, early Sunday morning, after the hell of the basement and the shootout, with hell still following him—he had been taken to Highland Hospital, then to the Alameda County Courthouse where the police forced him to lie on the floor while he was being booked, his wounded leg aching, his life a shambles. Hell kept after him as police took him to the San Quentin Hospital, where a guard pushed him down a flight of stairs, according to Robert Scheer in his introduction to *Post-Prison Writings*. Where *was* Eldridge this night? Astray again? Or still astray?

A photograph in Gene Marine's *The Black Panthers*, of an Oakland police officer in the foreground, seated with a shotgun across his legs, and in the background, Eldridge, has captured a unique moment of that night. They are in a police ambulance, en route whether from Highland Hospital to the county courthouse or to San

Quentin, I don't know—but Eldridge is in prison whites and his handcuffed arms are raised as he wipes the index finger of his right hand across his nose. There is a faraway look in his eyes, and I wonder—where was Eldridge at that moment in his times? I wonder if he knew. I think not. I'm glad World Wide Photos snapped that shot. It is a commentary on what Eldridge had written. "I had gone astray."

CHAPTER FIVE

THE EXODUS

Eldridge had come a long way since prison days. He still had a long way to go. His next stop was prison. San Quentin—his old stomping grounds.

He was in bad physical shape. The leg gunshot wound wasn't the worst of his agonies. Kathleen saw him " . . . sitting in a wheelchair with half his hair burned out. . . ." Gene Marine says he saw Eldridge a few hours after the shooting, apparently before Eldridge was hauled off to San Quentin, "shot . . . blinded with tear gas . . . his eyes still virtually swollen shut. . . ." It had been a long, long night, and he was hurting.

Eldridge was in bad parole shape, too. The California Adult Authority revoked his parole—without any required hearing, without warning, almost without notification. They said he was guilty of possessing a rifle, assault, associating with companions of bad reputation and of failing to cooperate with his parole officer. His parole officers had been right: higher authorities would revoke his parole at the first pretext. The night of April 6th gave them plenty of cause. And the Adult Authority had absolute dictatorship over prisoners and parolees.

So, although Eldridge's friends had quickly raised the $50,000 bail imposed, he still couldn't go free. The parole revocation notification came down the line even before daybreak.

Of course, Eldridge denied all the parole board's charges. His attorneys went to bat for him and succeeded, before Solano County (where the Vacaville Medical Facility is located) Superior Court Judge Raymond J. Sherwin, in getting a remarkable decision. It took time, but when it was rendered, Judge Sherwin's decision read in part:

"The record here is that though the petitioner was arrested and his parole canceled more than two months ago, hearings before the Adult Authority have not even been scheduled. There is nothing to indicate why it was deemed necessary to cancel his parole before his trial on the pending of criminal charges of which he is presumed innocent. . . .

"It has to be stressed that the uncontradicted evidence presented to this court indicated that the petitioner had been a model parolee. The peril to his parole status stemmed from no failure of personal rehabilitation, but from his undue eloquence in pursuing political goals, goals which were offensive to many of his contemporaries. Not only was there absence of cause for the cancellation of parole, it was the product of a type of pressure unbecoming, to say the least, of the law enforcement paraphernalia of this State. . . ."

Thus granted the writ of habeas corpus on June 12, 1968, Eldridge was free again.

* * * *

However, the borrowed time that Eldridge felt he was starting to live on when he assumed the Black Panther leadership following Newton's arrest was disappearing. He had said he wanted to do as much as possible before time ran out—well, this was June. He dived back into all that he still felt had to be done.

Newton's trial was scheduled for July. Eldridge pumped up the "Free Huey!" campaign, and when the trial started, the lawns around the Alameda County Courthouse building in Oakland were jammed with black-jacketed Panthers and hundreds of supporters chanting the campaign phrase and raising clenched fists. Kathleen spoke. Eldridge spoke. For days the courthouse grounds at the end of Lake Merritt and across from a little park thronged with the crowds.

There was also his presidential campaign to attend to. He did this eagerly despite his realization he would never win. Campaigning gave him all the more chance to speak his vehemence, which by now, in the light of his maltreatment by the parole board after the April 6th affair, was whipped to blacker rage than ever.

In a way, I wonder if Eldridge subconsciously didn't purposely *make* his time run out. Nobody in his right mind would be doing all that he was doing or saying all that he was saying. An ex-con, still battling with the parole authorities (they appealed Judge Sherwin's decision), with several felony counts liable to drop on him if the authorities won, running for the president of the United States, leading a crusade for an accused murderer who was the leader of a band of blacks threatening to overthrow the government—what kind of sense did all of that make? It was crazy, man. What was worse, he took on everybody in his new harangues—including Governor Reagan, the man who wielded the power of the parole board which was trying to put him back in prison. Talk about baiting the tiger. . . .

And all of this in the aftermath of yet another assassination of one more famous American. Senator Robert Kennedy had died in Los Angeles June 6th and his alleged assassin, Sirhan Sirhan, was in custody. The nation was grieving for the second time in about two months. Senator Kennedy's death also came on an anniversary important to Eldridge—exactly two months after the April 6th shoot out. He had spent that time in jail.

The police were still after the Panthers, some of them more brazen about it than others. On September 11, two Oakland police officers, off duty, shot and shattered the windows of the Panther headquarters on 56th and Grove. They were later fired over the incident, a reluctant act (in Panther eyes) on the part of Oakland Police Chief Charles Gains, but most welcomed by Panthers.

Eldridge's speeches increased in frequency and vehemence once he learned that the Adult Authority in appealing his release had succeeded in overturning Judge Sherwin's decision. He was now to report back to prison November 27, 1968. That was a strange quirk in legal processing, giving him some sixty days to report in. But it did one thing: it let Eldridge know exactly how quickly the small balance of his borrowed time was running out.

As far back as May 13. from the medical facility in Vacaville, he had written an open letter to Governor Reagan, letting things all hang out again as he always did, telling the governor how he felt about the parole authority's behavior and about a lot of things. He compared the Oakland Police Department ". . . to the racist police in Mississippi and South Africa. . . ."

He told Governor Reagan that he was finished with the Adult Authority ". . . with parole officers, with prisons, and all of their world of restraint, confinement and punishment. I can't relate to them anymore, because I am free. I am a free man, Governor, and I no longer know how to submit and play the part of a debtor to society. What I owe to society is the work that I must do outside these stone walls. My work can't wait, it won't wait, it should not wait. And you, Governor, should welcome me back to my job, because I was dealing with some of the most pressing problems facing not only the State of California but this nation and the world. . . . And the people you can't reach . . . are the very people with whom I am on the best of terms, for I am of them, I am one of them. . . . The bottom of the world is in motion, Governor, and Bobby Dylan's 'empty handed beggar' is at the door, except that his hand is not empty any more. He's got a gun in that hand. And he's stopped begging. . . . When he finally stops talking altogether, he is going to start shooting. . . ."

As the fall quarter opened at the University of California, Eldridge was asked to teach an experimental sociology course on the Berkeley campus. The course was to deal with racism, and Oakland Police Chief Charles Gains and others had agreed, suprisingly, to be participating speakers along with

154

Eldridge. Although the academic senate approved the course, the regents, at Governor Reagan's persuasion, and contrary to established procedures, balked. This made a new issue for Eldridge to tie into. In the increasingly frequent speeches he was asked to make, he now referred to this issue, calling the governor, "Mickey Mouse Reagan."

Time was running short, so the teaching issue was not as important as it seemed. This isn't to downgrade the principle involved; I mean time was more of the essence than teaching at UC. But he never let audiences forget his opinions of the men who ran California's government and the nation's.

To students at Stanford on October 1, he opened a speech with "I want to thank . . . Mickey Mouse Reagan and Donald Duck Rafferty (the State Superintendent of Education) for making it possible [for him to speak]. . . ."

After making numerous points he asked for everyone's vote in the upcoming November election: "Good white people, you've got to support me. George Wallace, you've got to support me, Law and Order Nixon, you've got to support me, Meathead Me-too Humphrey, you've got to support me—or else the niggers are going to come into the white suburbs and turn the white suburbs into shooting galleries."

Then he added, shockingly, ". . . I'm not here campaigning for your vote. Because I wouldn't give a d— if you didn't go to the polls in November. As a matter of fact, if you're going to vote for one of those pigs, I would strongly recommend that you didn't go. . . ."

Time finally shortened to just five days. November

22, 1968, found Eldridge speaking in San Francisco on behalf of his defense.

"Good evening," he began. "Kind of stuck for words tonight. I don't know whether this is a hello or a goodbye. I talked to my parole officer today, and he told me that on Wednesday the 27th he wanted me to call him up about 8:30 in the morning, so he could tell me where to meet him so he could transport me to San Quentin. They want to have a parole revocation hearing. . . .

"Rehabilitation in . . . California is less than a bad joke. . . . I've had more trouble out of parole officers and the Department of Corrections simply because I've been relating to the Movement than I had when I was committing robberies, rapes and other things that I didn't get caught for. . . .

"There's something more dangerous about attacking the pigs of the power structure verbally than there is in walking into the Bank of America with a gun and attacking it forthrightly. Bankers hate armed robbery, but someone who stands up and directly challenges their racist system, that drives them crazy. . . ."

"I don't know how to go about waiting until people start practicing what they preach . . . because all I see is a very critical situation, a chaotic situation where there's pain, there's suffering, there's death, and I see no justification for waiting until tomorrow to say what you could say tonight. . . ."

Toward the close he talked about the impending return to prison. "I cannot relate to spending the next four years in the penitentiary, not with madmen with supreme power in their hands. . . . My heart is out here with the people who are trying to improve our environment. . . ."

That was his final speech, a kind of farewell address.

Two days later, a Sunday, he had dinner in a San Francisco Chinatown restaurant with Robert Scheer, a former editor of *Ramparts* who later ran unsuccessfully for Congress. Afterwards, en route across Columbus Street to the La Tosca for a *cappuccino*, they stopped to let a red light change, when a patrol car screeched to a halt and two cops jumped out heading for Eldridge with their hands on their holsters.

"What did you call us?" they shouted, according to Scheer's recollection.

Eldridge said nothing, recognizing the tactic of provocation. But Scheer stepped in, also aware of the behavior, and with much demonstration of proper identification, succeeded in sending the police on their way without any more strenuous trouble.

Afterwards, Scheer remembers, in his introduction to *Post-Prison Writings*, Eldridge told him that if he (Eldridge) had been walking alone, he would have been killed.

"And," said Scheer, "from what I had seen of those swollen police faces, I knew he was right."

And that was last time he saw Eldridge, Scheer said.

* * * *

It isn't hard to imagine what thoughts muscled their way through Eldridge's mind in the closing hours of his "borrowed time." He had wrestled with everybody, all the political powers, all the community forces, all the ideological might.

157

The cops were persistently after him and now the FBI was involved. The conspiracy that existed in the country was not only one of black revolutionaries seeking to overthrow the government, but, Eldridge was convinced, equally one of men in higher authority, racists and others, misunderstanding the black cause and combining their powers to squash anyone wanting to change the traditional ways.

He had battled the University of California, even Governor Reagan—indeed, was still doing so. The lecture series in the sociology class at the Berkeley campus had finally been allowed, but students were to get no credit for it; his seventh lecture was coming up in two days, and he had little heart for it.

He was senior editor at *Ramparts*, to be sure, but even that was a battleground now with his parole revocation appeal still in the judicial mill. His appeal was in the hands of U.S. Supreme Court Justice Thurgood Marshall who was deciding whether the court should take the case. Parole or prison—that was the key factor. For the April 6th episode he was charged with criminal acts, but he—as well as the public, more and more—knew it was a political matter. He was a political target more than anything else, which added injustice upon injustice when you consider the Constitution freedoms supposedly allowed a man for his political beliefs.

He had even run for the presidency of the United States (well, not for the *presidency;* as he told an interviewer in Algiers later in 1969, "I was running for the revolutionary movement. . . ." The campaign offered a forum for getting revolutionary views to larger numbers of people). That had been futile from the beginning. Despite his being barred from the California ballot though, he managed to gather in some thirty thousand votes. The man who won, Richard Nixon, was as hardcore a law-and-order militant as Eldridge was a black revolutionary liberationist. Eldridge would later add Nixon to his name-calling list as an "underdeveloped . . . political and moral cretin. . . ."

Huey Newton was still undergoing trial. How successful had all the efforts on his behalf been?

And Eldridge's private life had become a state of siege. With Kathleen just as fiery a Black Panther as himself, their home had turned into an armed camp.

Was it all worth it? Oh, yes. But time was gone.

A glimpse into his thinking comes from an article by Henry E. Weinstein in the January 20, 1969, issue of the liberal *Nation* magazine. Weinstein, a third-year law student at the University of California who had written about the Newton case for the *Daily Californian*, the student newspaper, and who had been a member of the student delegation before Governor Reagan on Eldridge's controversial lecture series, had visited Eldridge that Sunday afternoon before Eldridge had gone to dinner with Robert Scheer.

Weinstein had been accompanied by a friend, Dan Lang, who brought along a copy of *Soul on Ice* for Eldridge to autograph. Eldridge wrote in the flyleaf: "For Dan Lang. On a Sunday afternoon, the Sunday of Sundays for me. Perhaps my last Sunday. I don't know. No matter what, however, the truth is still the truth and the struggle must and will go on. All power to the people. The spirit of the people is greater than man's technology."

Weinstein wrote his impression on entering Eldridge's home that afternoon. "As I entered . . . and watched the double-bolted door close behind me, I was more than ever impressed by the fact that Cleaver had made a leap that is characteristic of the true revolutionary. He had put his life on the line for his beliefs. . . ."

They talked a bit about the university lectures, grimly titled "Dehumanization and Regeneration in the American Social Order." And about students—black and white:

". . . Almost all black college students," Eldridge spoke into Weinstein's tape recorder, "are from the black bourgeoisie. The black middle class are the most alienated from their roots; when the idea of black consciousness began to develop they had the furthest to go. . . ."

This made for problems, ". . . the compartmentalization of black college students. They have been viewed as a separate entity, but they must be seen as part of the larger community. . . ."

White students were no different, he told Weinstein: ". . . This goes for white students as well. They have been compartmentalized themselves too. Liberation must come and can only come from the entire community, not just from the colleges."

Back in that cell on the honor block at Folsom Prison he had written of his faith in the younger generation. Eldridge hadn't changed; his faith still resided in the nation's youth. Nor had he changed his belief that hatred would solve nothing, that racism wasn't the problem—humanity, black and white, was the problem.

American humanity also faced the problem of guilt: ". . . the guilt problem is part of the racial heritage of America. But such guilt feelings make many people nonfunctional from our point of view. . . ."

And he repeated to Weinstein what he had told his San Francisco audience a few days before, that he was supposed to call his parole officer at eight thirty Wednesday morning. "I am planning on continuing my daily life as normal. I will give my scheduled lecture on Tuesday at the university. . . . We will have to wait and see. . . ."

The parole revocation hearing scheduled for Wednesday was obviously a kind of "end of the line," the last tick of the clock.

"I may be cut off from the movement here. . . ." he said, then added an afterthought, ". . . let the struggle continue. It should intensify, come hell or high water."

And, as always in time of crises, when all the conflicting inner thoughts somersault over each other, Eldridge's determination led him to say, "I'm not going to say goodbye because I'm not gone."

But on Tuesday the last legal maneuver by his attorney Charles Garry (whom Panthers had dubbed "the first white Black Panther") to avoid Eldridge's return to prison was thwarted. U.S. Supreme Court Justice Thurgood Marshall, the only Negro on the high court, flatly refused to grant Eldridge a stay of his return to prison. He offered no comment.

And so, on Wednesday, November 27, 1968,

Eldridge was gone. He had slipped quietly beyond everyone's reach.

That day's *Oakland Tribune* carried two stories. One, in a banner across the front page above the paper's name, had the paper-selling headline: "INSIDE CLEAVER'S FORTRESS—HE'S GONE."

Below, Bill Bancroft's by-lined story of his visit to Eldridge's home began, "Eldridge Cleaver is not at home at 2777 Pine St., San Francisco."

Inside, another story declared that an all-points bulletin had been issued for this arrest. The next day's *San Francisco Chronicle* said the bulletin had been issued by the Adult Authority ninety minutes after Eldridge had failed to show up at their offices in the state building. The *Chronicle's* story ran alongside one about the closing of the embattled San Francisco State College campus.

The *Tribune's* Bancroft had toured the Cleaver home with Kathleen and defense attorney Garry. The home was a narrow three-story Victorian frame structure, the ground floor of which was occupied by the landlord and the upper two stories by Eldridge and Kathleen—and a host of armed blacks.

Throughout the house, Garry was careful to show Bancroft—that doors had been reinforced by placing a steel plate between two pieces of plywood a "plywood sandwich," for protection against attack from police, or anyone else.

The armed youthful guards were stationed at strategic points everywhere, Garry pointing out because "we don't want any rough stuff or anybody shooting in here."

Garry had taken Bancroft aside after an earlier press

conference to show him that Eldridge truly was not around. "We don't want any excuses for the police to come in here and have any trouble," he said.

Later, one officer, unarmed, was allowed in for a similar inspection; by then, though, Kathleen had ordered the guards also to strip themselves of their weapons.

Neither Kathleen nor Garry knew of Eldridge's whereabouts. Kathleen said she hadn't seen her husband "since Sunday."

She told the *Chronicle* that she didn't think he had fled the United States as some rumors already maintained.

Garry had talked to Eldridge Sunday, but had not seen him since the previous Thursday. He said he still intended "to represent him, no matter what."

Kathleen, of course, voiced similar loyalty: "I'll stand by him. I want to remain married to him even if he goes to prison for five years."

Other reports noted that Eldridge had not been seen for two days. He had not shown up for his seventh—and next-to-last—lecture at UC. Kathleen had gone there, expecting to meet him. The press had been invited for the first time, and some five hundred students had showed up. The class that day was scheduled for a special event—a citation, presented to Kathleen in Eldridge's absence, by Professor Owen Chamberlain, a Nobel laureate in physics, signed by forty faculty members praising Eldridge for "continuing to appear under very difficult circumstances."

Eldridge's parole officer, Stanley Carter, had been unable to contact him, but said, before the ultimate realization finally struck, "He's always cooperated in

163

the past, and I expect he will now."

But with Justice Marshall's decision the clock stopped. Eldridge's last option had gone. Time for cooperation had also gone. When the time came for him to report Wednesday, November 27, 1968, he was gone.

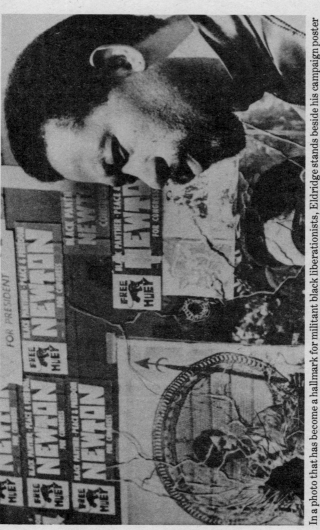

In a photo that has become a hallmark for militant black liberationists, Eldridge stands beside his campaign poster (he was a candidate for president on the Peace and Freedom Party ticket) on September 10, 1968. Huey Newton's picture, on the left, and Eldridge's had been fired on by angry Oakland police officers. Newton was in jail, convicted of voluntary manslaughter in the death of an Oakland policeman. *Wide World Photos.*

On August 22, 1969, Eldridge was a fugitive in Algeria. Here he addresses a news conference in Algiers on the occasion of the opening of a Black Panther liaison office. Kathleen is to his immediate left. As part of his remarks that day, he backed the Arab struggle against Israel. *Wide World Photos.*

By late 1969, none of these Black Panther leaders was free in the United States. Eldridge, minister of information, was in Algeria. Huey Newton, minister of defense, (upper left) was in prison. Bobby Seale, national chairman, (center left) was in jail on a contempt of court conviction. And Fred Hampton, Illinois Panther leader, (lower left) was slain in a Chicago gun battle. *Wide World Photos*.

In October, 1970, Eldridge welcomed Dr. Timothy Leary at Algiers airport upon Leary's arrival after his escape from jail in California. *Wide World Photos.*

In 1977 Eldridge and Kathleen were in Dallas, Texas, on location with a television crew filming part of a television campaign sponsored by the Baptist General Convention of Texas. *Religious News Service Photo.*

Also in 1977, Dr. Robert Schuller, pastor of the Garden Grove, California, Community Church, invited Eldridge to join him, Corrie ten Boom, and Charles Colson (left) during the Sunday morning service. The trio was invited to testify to the congregation and to illustrate Dr. Schuller's sermon, "How to Climb Down a Mountain without Falling." *Religious News Service Photo.*

BOOK THREE

THE EXILE

CHAPTER ONE

CUBA

Once the hubbub of Eldridge's disappearance died down, rumors concerning his whereabouts sprouted up like weeds. By Saturday, November 30th, Charles Raudebaugh was writing in the *San Francisco Chronicle* that the search for him "swung suddenly to Canada yesterday," in spite of Eldridge's attorney's repeated comments that he had "no idea" of where his client was, and of Kathleen's insistence that she believed her husband still somewhere in the Bay Area.

Raudebaugh wrote that "lawmen said the Cleaver was reported to be" one of sixty-eight passengers aboard a chartered plane bound for Montreal for a meeting called the Hemispheric Conference to End the War in Vietnam. Delegates from Cuba and other Central American countries as well as the United States and Canada were supposed to be attending. The information was reliable enough that Deputy State Attorney General Edward O'Brien said his office had asked federal authorities for a fugitive warrant.

"This is the same action we take for any other

hoodlum," O'Brien was quoted as saying.

The U.S. attorney in San Francisco, Cecil Poole, declined to issue the warrant, though, until the state provided further details.

As a matter of fact, Eldridge was in Montreal, his first touchdown in exile. Eight years later, after his voluntary return, he admitted the sardonic pleasure he had enjoyed watching TV in Canada as the officials searched through his abandoned home on Pine Street in San Francisco. It gave him a "funny feeling" of amusement, he said.

He wasn't in Montreal long. Within a few short months he would be discovered in Cuba. Picking up the stories appearing in newspapers, *Time* magazine reported in its May 30, 1969, issue a dispatch from James Pringle, the Havana correspondent for Reuters, that he had visited Eldridge in a sixth-floor apartment of an "unpretentious apartment building near the heart of Havana." The beard Eldridge had reportedly shaved off to alter his appearance had since grown back and he had gained weight. The Reuters correspondent also reported that Eldridge was working on a sequel to *Soul on Ice*.

A week later *U.S. News & World Report* added that Eldridge was "living simply, not engaging in politics. The U.S. asked Swiss diplomats to check his status."

This report also noted that Kathleen was expecting a child in July and that the $50,000 bail Eldridge had forfeited by fleeing was due to be returned to the bail bondsman by June 23. Eldridge's friends back home had to pay that.

* * * *

That Eldridge was in Havana is not surprising. Back in 1967, Fidel Castro had publicly embraced Stokely Carmichael at the OLAS Congress of Latin American revolutionaries, thus endorsing the American black revolutionary cause. He pledged Cuba's full backing of Carmichael's black power people. Knowing this, Eldridge's strategy was to keep alive the cause at home by opening up a Black Panther Party information office in Cuba and establishing liaison with all the other numerous black revolutionary and liberationist groups there. But by the time he got to Havana, Cuba's situation had been changed drastically. Che Guevara had been killed in Bolivia. Cuba's revolutionary-support program had been sidetracked and the country was trying to solve its domestic economic problems by producing millions of tons of sugar to balance its budget. With internal problems Cuba didn't want to make unnecessary international waves.

When Eldridge arrived, the Cubans let him know he was welcome and could remain as long as he wanted but that he could not pursue any political activity for a while. The forced inactivity was as confining to Eldridge as a prison cell. He languished, grew restive, discovered games the Cubans were playing and became increasingly disenchanted.

The turnabout from the frenetic activity in the states to inaction in Cuba began to work other results in Eldridge, too. New pressures, although much different from the harassment in the Bay Area, began to exert their toll.

For one thing, he was increasingly anxious about Kathleen. He knew she was pregnant and that the Cubans had promised her safe transport into exile.

In putting together the sequence of Eldridge's exile, I reread free-lance writer-photographer Lee Lockwood's *Conversation with Eldridge Cleaver—Algiers* (Dell Publishing Co., 1970), and some of Lockwood's comments brought home again to me the *person* of Eldridge which so many writers from time to time have perceived during interviews with him. They show the effects of his exile on him even after the short five months that had passed from his disappearance up to May, 1969, when Lockwood ran across Eldridge in Havana by accident.

Lockwood arrived there on a totally different assignment. At the airport he was surprised when asked if he would like to meet Eldridge. He said yes, definitely, and set up arrangements.

Before getting into the significant things he noticed about Eldridge, Lockwood describes his first sight of the exiled Panther striding down a Havana street en route to meet him. It's an interesting aside. Eldridge lived only a few blocks from where Lockwood was staying at the Hotel Nacional and Lockwood hoped to meet him at the corner and shorten Eldridge's walk.

"In the midst of [this] genial hubbub, I picked out Eldridge clearly a block away. He was a head taller than all the Cubans in sight and dressed in sandals without socks (in Cuba, sandals are worn barefoot only by women, homosexuals and foreigners), baby-blue jeans, and a pink gaucho shirt which the late afternoon sun lit up as startlingly as if it had been dyed in Day-Glo paint. He moved down the opposite sidewalk at a leisurely pace halfway between a stroll and a prowl, his powerful shoulders erect, his head thrust forward a bit, his eyes invisible behind dark green shades. His black

Oriental beard, which, according to rumor, he had shaved off when leaving the United States, seemed fully restored. . . ."

Eldridge's appearance on that Havana street was far different from his black Black Panther attire which had been sometimes accentuated by baby-blue turtlenecks. But always he stood out, carrying his six-foot-two frame erect and forceful. In Havana, as Lockwood saw, Eldridge was far less rigid, more relaxed as he sauntered to their first meeting.

At their first encounter, he detected a reserve in Eldridge: ". . . When you sit down to dinner with Eldridge Cleaver, you know you are sitting with a black man. He *is black*, and he makes you think about it; in fact, he never lets you forget it. He is black and you are white.

"This understanding was communicated with neither hostility nor arrogance, simply in the spirit of recognition—a fact that had to be accepted before a relationship was possible. Though I found this to be a little disconcerting at first . . . nevertheless, I think I ultimately felt more at ease with Cleaver because of this implicit confrontation.

"I was also surprised to learn, as I grew to know him better, that the reserve I had sensed in him at the beginning was not, as I had supposed, merely strategic. It was partly that, but beyond tactics lay the reticence of a naturally shy person, an elementally human quality that I found touching then and even more so later when I reread some of his more aggressive published rhetoric.

"At the same time, he projected, beneath the mild exterior, a feeling of great strength—but strength under hair-trigger tension. He was enormously moody. At times he seemed like a man pursued and harried by demons visible only to himself. He had buried alive within him great reserves of anger, ready to explode on slight provocation. I found him one of the most complex and tormented men I have ever met. He seemed to hold within his mind a vast oscillating field of contradictory impulses. These were mirrored in his behavior: alternately he would be shrewd and naive, tough-minded and soft-hearted, indolent and dynamic, thoughtful and impulsive, indecisive and determined, idealistic and cynical, self-confident and unsure.

"I do not know how much of this torment was caused by the circumstances in which he found himself, but I suspect they were a considerable factor, for, as I shall explain in a moment, he was under enormous pressure in Cuba. Whatever the case, Cleaver 'went through a lot of changes,' as he himself often remarked with characteristic candor. Even on first meeting he fearlessly exposed all the facets of his character, rough and smooth, with no apologies. I think it was this quality of existential toughness in Cleaver that impressed me most. . . ."

I have to agree with Lockwood. I have known Eldridge only on the "other side of the fence," so to speak, since his return from exile, since his conversion to Christ, and through reading his writings. But my face-to-face meetings, and our phone conversations, have always contained much of what Lockwood noticed. I have sensed many of the same qualities Lockwood sensed, although I have seen a different Eldridge from the man exposed in those Cuban years. He is a softer man, not softer in strength, never that, but gentler in his relating to others. That part of Eldridge was forgotten in all the tumult after his parole in 1966—in fact, forgotten by himself, in the shadow of all the glare of the public image focused on in his book and his Panther activities.

* * * *

Time on one's hands leads a man to introspection. He has opportunity to reassess himself, reevaluate himself and his objectives, come to terms with himself. Such times more often than we realize are given to us for just this purpose.

Eldridge was being forced into this kind of situation. It would last for years. In Cuba it brought him into conflict with his own impatience to be on the work of the party liaison, his anxiety over Kathleen, his estrangement from friends, the suspiciously deliberate delays of Cuban officials. He was finding nothing that he had consciously sought there. And he was beginning to find, although very subtly at first, that he was really seeking something beyond what he thought he had come hunting for. Thus the "vast oscillating field of contradictory impulses" Lockwood said he perceived to be in Eldridge's mind. Eldridge was already a torn man on his arrival; he was being torn daily by the inner contradictions and the outer frustrations of life in Cuba; he would be torn even more before his exile was ended.

* * * *

If nothing else, Eldridge missed friendship. Gene Marine, in his *The Black Panthers*, wrote of something Eldridge had mentioned to him shortly before his disappearance. The possibility of his having to return to prison was always foremost in his thinking during those days. Eldridge told Marine, "When I went back into prison before, it didn't matter, you know? Nobody cared anything about me anyway. . . .

"But this time—this time I've found something, you know, since I've been in the movement and working with all these cats. I've never had that before, never at all. I can't go back in there now and leave that out here. I've got friends—I've got friends for the first time in my life and man, I just don't think I can do without that anymore" (pp. 195-196).

All of these factors exerted their pressures on Eldridge—anxiety over his pregnant wife, the lack of friends who cared for him, great amounts of time that led to introspection, and his basic shyness that made him uncomfortable unless in familiar surroundings or with people he felt he could trust.

He had been given a tour of the island soon after his arrival, and his material needs were met. The Cubans put him up in a commodious apartment, gave him a cook and housekeeper, saw that his food and supplies were brought in, even provided him with a security man. Just whose security the latter was guarding, Eldridge's or Cuba's, seems questionable in retrospect, but his name was Silva and he was always around. But Eldridge was in virtual isolation; he had no car; his knowledge of Spanish only basic. His communications were cut off.

His first taste of what lay ahead came within a month or so after his arrival in Cuba in December, 1968. He heard that Bobby Seale and some other brothers were going to Sweden for some liberation conference and that the Cubans were also sending delegates. Eldridge asked the Cuban delegate to get word to Seale to come to Cuba after the Swedish affair, but when the man returned he happened to hand Eldridge some papers he shouldn't have seen. Even his rudimentary knowledge of Spanish told him that the delegate had been instructed to advise Seale that Eldridge did *not* think it appropriate that the brothers come to Cuba just then—which was totally untrue. Eldridge was antsy to get on with things. He did a doubletake, raised his eyebrows, but let it slide. Still, suspicions began to accumulate.

In the course of the following months, Eldridge began to meet some of the hijackers granted asylum in Cuba. One by one they fed him their own dissatisfactions. They felt that racism was just as existent there as back in the States. One hijacker, particularly, caused problems that distressed Eldridge and was instrumental in his final break with Castro and Cuba. An acquaintance of former prison days had heard Eldridge was in Cuba and made a plane-hijack dash for freedom. Once in Cuba, though, he was tossed in prison there, too. Undaunted, he made another dash, this time for Eldridge's apartment and arrived, panicked, just ahead of the local police. Eldridge took him in, refused the police entry, and thus drew down Cuban disfavor for providing asylum to an American while Eldridge himself was enjoying Cuban asylum. Distinctly it is not the way a foreigner should behave under the circumstances.

Stories of Eldridge's disenchantment began to filter back to the States. A United Press story out of Paris printed in the Berkeley *Gazette* December 1, 1969, months after Eldridge had left Cuba, told why one of his former aides, Earl Ferrell, had broken with Eldridge. The break occurred before Eldridge faced up to the truth about Cuba, but told in retrospect it gives the reason he finally left.

"Fidel Castro," said Ferrell, "has like created a dictatorship of white racists. And this is actually what they are."

Eldridge finally saw the Cuban white-racists power structure for what it was and left. Or was asked to leave, that is.

The Cubans manufactured his departure with all the subtle indirectness of some sly Oriental diplomacy. Before this occurred, though, Eldridge was learning through friendliness with some black musicians and entertainers that racist attitudes were prevalent throughout Cuban society. The most noticeable proofs were the lack of representation in the upper echelons of Castro's revolutionary leadership, discrimination in job advancement and prohibitions against various accouterments of black identity, such as Afro hairdos and clothing and the practice of traditional African religions. In the course of all these bits and pieces Eldridge could not help but note the same kind of hypocrisy in Cuba that he had ranted about in the States: America proclaimed democracy and equality for all but continued to suppress the blacks; Cuba proclaimed full support of the black liberation struggle abroad but completely disregarded the racial problem within its own borders.

Eldridge's growing insights became evident to the Cubans and they decided it was time for him to go. Not that he minded; it was the way they handled it which led him to erase them from his list of hopes. First he heard

Then the Reuters correspondent found him through the aid of an American woman with a Georgian drawl who had dreams that Castro would one day marry her, but who was becoming disenchanted herself and starting to play some kind of game of her own. The Reuters dispatch was played up on the front pages of American newspapers. This dismayed Cubans who thought Eldridge had collaborated with the correspondent.

Just days later Eldridge called Lee Lockwood to tell him that the Cubans were sending him to Algiers "in order to take the heat off Cuba," which by then was drawing international wrath by becoming a haven for skyjackers. The Cubans were seriously trying to improve their image, and when Eldridge provided sanctuary for his skyjacker friend whom they wanted back in their own prison, he became an obstacle to their intentions. Also, tired of Cuban delays in providing aid to bring American Panthers there, Eldridge began recruiting every Afro-American he could find to his Panther liaison headquarters in Havana. This compounded Cuban dismay. Officials designed Eldridge's trip to Algiers to "get some news coverage," advising him that he would be back in a few weeks.

So Eldridge asked Lockwood to find Kathleen, because he himself had to leave for Algiers right away. Lockwood agreed and fortunately hooked up with Kathleen in Paris, bound roundabout from New York to Cuba. He diverted her to Algiers as Eldridge had asked. But when Eldridge arrived in Algiers he was told he was only there to pick up Kathleen, that the Algerians had changed their minds about whatever it was, and that now Eldridge was supposed to go to in May that Kathleen was at last on her way to Havana.

Amman, Jordan, to tour some Palestinian camps. This struck a sour note with Eldridge; what was he going to do in Jordan with a wife who was eight months pregnant?

The Cubans in Algiers also told Eldridge to stay away from an American woman suspected of being a CIA agent. So disgusted was he with the Cubans by then that Eldridge did just the opposite; he contacted her and found she was organizing the Pan-African Conference in Algeria. She could have been CIA Chief Richard Helms' private secretary for all Eldridge cared at the moment. It turned out that Eldridge's name was on her list but that she had not known how to contact him. Now that he was in Algiers, he should stay and attend the Pan-African Conference. He did. And the Cuban part of his long exile was over. Eldridge felt he was well rid of Fidel Castro and his island cradle of black liberationist nonsupport.

CHAPTER TWO

ALGIERS

Eldridge entered Algiers in secret. The Algerians did not grant him permission to publicize his presence until some time later. He had come with considerable enthusiasm, despite the strange boot out the door Cuba had given him, because it meant reunion with Kathleen after nearly eight months and because Algiers was the focal point for the Third World milieu. But his enthusiasm was dampened by the unsettling behavior of Algerian officials whose brand of red tape in many ways was more frustrating than the kind he had encountered back in the States.

In fact, when Lee Lockwood arrived for an interview two weeks after Eldridge, in late June, he noted that Eldridge's physical living conditions were worse than in Cuba. The Cleavers were staying at the Victoria Hotel, which Lockwood said was a place that should "never be listed in any tourist's guide to the city—except as a hotel to be strictly avoided." It was located on a narrow side street in what was once the Arab quarter, just off one of downtown Algiers busiest

179

streets and only a few blocks from the harbor.

"The Cleavers were installed," Lockwood wrote in *Conversation with Eldridge Cleaver—Algiers* (pp. 24-25) "in a small room on the fourth floor of this sleazy establishment in the most uncomfortable circumstances imaginable. Most of the room was filled by twin beds, which jutted out from the wall almost to the windows. Crowded into the remaining space were a dilapidated armoire packed to overflowing with clothes and with garments also hanging on its doors, a number of trunks and suitcases, and several small tables and chairs, through all of which one had to pick his way to get to the other side of the room. In a corner, behind a shabby curtain, there was a shower, but the toilet was outside in the hall. Every available inch of surface was covered with something: not only a melange of books, magazines, more clothing, and Kathleen's cosmetics but also such equipment as a large stereo phonograph, an expensive tape recorder, and a combined radio-and-cassette-recorder—all apparently recent acquisitions.

"Kathleen, nearing her *accouchement*, was suffering from a combination of physical exhaustion and nervous tension and was confined to her bed most of the time. There being no restaurant or kitchen in the hotel, Eldridge ate all of his meals outside and brought back food for his wife in a stack of interlocking aluminum lunch pails he had bought in a sporting goods store in town. Since they were on their own and not the guests of the government, they were running short of money. In addition, there was great uncertainty about where Kathleen would have her baby, now due in a matter of only weeks."

Eldridge's entry permit had expired and in spite of his having been there for over two weeks he had still been unable to see "a single government official for a clarification of his status. There was serious question as to whether he would be permitted to remain in the country even clandestinely. Until this problem could be resolved, he was obliged to stay under cover, especially out of sight of the many American tourists and businessmen who thronged the city. . . ."

If the Cubans had been dilatory and evasive and in the end openly inhospitable, the Algerians at first displayed an almost total unconcern for Eldridge. They only wanted him to remain in virtual hiding.

* * * *

Lee Lockwood's interview with Eldridge in late June, 1969, is the most succinct I've been able to find on Eldridge's thinking at that time. It wasn't published until 1970, by which time numerous stories from widely separated sources were being published in the States. Excerpts will show where Eldridge's thinking was and where it appeared headed as he began the second stage of his long exile.

They talked a lot of political theory, but Eldridge got into specific aspects of the struggle back home. He was convinced a "conspiratorial blueprint" was becoming clear between President Nixon's new administration and the FBI—continuing his earlier thinking about police harassment. Now it was being refined, perfected. Inflated bail was being imposed on arrested blacks—$100,000 and $200,000. This, in the face of constitutional restraints against unreasonable bail, "for some poor cat out of the ghetto," was "ransom," Eldridge said. The move to "destroy" the Black Panther Party, which party leaders had claimed from 1967 on, "has escalated."

Eldridge thought this "persecution . . . this blatant persecution, these open fascistic police tactics under the Nixon administration, will not only swell the membership of the Black Panther Party but will increase the ranks of all radical and revolutionary organizations in the United States, because people will recognize that if such things can be done in the black community, they can be done in the white community, too. . . ."

His favorite expression for the United States was "Babylon" because ". . . of all the symbols that I've ever run across to indicate a decadent society, I find the term Babylon, which I take from Revelation in the Bible, to be the most touching. That's how they describe Babylon—as a decadent society. . . . I don't want to peddle the Bible. But it comes out of the Bible anyway, out of Revelation. . . ."

Lockwood asked Eldridge how he felt now, in 1969, about what he had written after Martin Luther King's assassination, that King's murder marked the end of nonviolence and that "the bloody struggle starts now . . . a bloodbath and a guerrilla war." Did Eldridge think a guerrilla war was absolutely necessary? Were the Black Panthers making such plans as many were rumoring?

Eldridge maneuvered away from implicating the Panthers that way but said that what was necessary, what he was dedicated to and what a lot of people were dedicated to is ". . . to recognize that we have to fight a revolutionary struggle for the violent overthrow of the United States government and the total destruction of the racist, capitalist, imperialist, neo-colonialist power structure.

"This is what I'll be working on henceforth: to establish the North American Liberation Front, which will include the revolutionary forces in every community. It will not be an all-black organization; it will be a machinery that will include the revolutionaries in the white community . . . and all other ethnic, minority communities. . . .

"I'm saying to you that I feel that the United States as it exists today has to be totally obliterated and has to be rebuilt and restructured, and the wealth, the means of production, the entire system, has to be rearranged. And it won't be rearranged peacefully . . . because . . . those who control the United States have no intention of modifying what's going on there. . . ."

He noted sardonically that the power structure back home considered him a fugitive from justice. ". . . Well, as far as *I* am concerned, *they* are fugitives from the justice of the people. . . . I intend to do everything I can to see to it that what I represent and what I advocate prevails."

The U.S. struggle was not ". . . an isolated struggle. . . ." But Eldridge considered ". . . my battlefront, the battlefront where I can make the best contribution because of my familiarity with it, is in Babylon. This is where I want to fight. This is where I want to die."

Did that mean he was going back to the United States?

"That means I'm going back. That means I have every intention of going back. . . .

". . . You see, I believe that there are two Americas. There is the America of the American dream, and there is the America of the American nightmare. I feel that I am a citizen of the American dream, and that the revolutionary struggle of which I am a part is a struggle against the American nightmare. . . .

"The children of America are the ones I consider to be the citizens of the American dream. First . . . the ideals . . . the Bill of Rights . . . the Constitution . . . the Lord's Prayer . . . these things that have inspired people everywhere . . . are implanted in the minds of the children of America. This is the foundation of the American character.

"But here is when the trick comes in. Later on, these ideals are twisted to function in behalf of a vicious power structure and a vicious economic and political and social system. My quarrel is against what is done with this foundation that has been instilled in people. . . .

"I believe that the American dream is just as it says, 'that all men are created equal, and that they are endowed by their Creator'—I mean, I don't believe in God, you know, but I understand what the thought is—'that they are endowed by their Creator with certain inalienable (sic) rights, and that among these are the rights of life, liberty and the pursuit of happiness.' And not the pursuit of property, which was struck from that. . . .

"For instance, take the Pledge of Allegiance. . . . I

184

remember as a child how I used to choke up every morning—we used to have to line up and pledge allegiance. . . . Now it didn't say 'I pledge allegiance to racism, to capitalism, to the war in Vietnam, and to imperialism and neo-colonialism, and J. Edgar Hoover, and Richard Nixon, and Ronald Reagan, and Mayor Alioto, and the Tactical Squad, and Mace, and billy clubs, and dead niggers on the street shot by pigs.' I mean it didn't say that. . . ."

Ideologically, although Eldridge's hopes indicated a socialist America, a communist America. ". . . I'm not saying a Russian America; I'm not saying a Chinese America; I'm not saying a Cuban America; I'm saying an American application of the principles of socialism that hopes to move to the classless society. . . . We have to make a specific application of the general principles of socialism to the American situation and come up with a Yankee-Doodle-Dandy version of socialism, one that will fit our particular situation. I'm saying we have to do away with the institution of private property. . . ."

The way he saw things was that revolution was coming. He prophesied (not from any visions, but just from his assessment of conditions) that ". . . by 1972 we will have a military coup in the United States and a military dictatorship, because by that time there will be a full-scale war going on . . . and an election for the presidency will be out of the question." Everybody—"the pigs of the power structure and the revolutionaries . . ." would find an election out of the question.

A war was already going on, with ". . . the enemy . . . killing more . . . victims, and the victims killing . . . more of the enemy. . . . These things have a way of escalating overnight. . . ."

As to the kind of institutions or society that would be created afterwards, Eldridge didn't have everything worked out, but "once the revolution is secured against all forms of counterrevolution," it would be necessary to create new organizations all down the line ". . . so that people can participate in the discussions that are going on and can have their will counted when the decisions are being made." He admitted no society he had ever studied was perfect, but did have an idea of utopia in his head. He would eliminate "the crisis between men and women in Babylon" by engineering something to handle the "magnetism between male and female" so that people could function better.

He believed that man is basically good, but balked at Lockwood's asking him if he believed in the "perfectibility of man" as being an extremism. "I don't believe that you have to show" people the way to be good, ". . . you just have to get out of their way, you know? . . . You don't have to teach a flower or bud how to bloom. You just have to let it live . . . you don't have to teach people how to be human. I think you have to teach them how to stop being inhuman."

Lockwood finally wound the interview down beyond individuals to Eldridge himself. How was he looking forward to becoming a father?

Eldridge was as perplexed as any expectant father, and as delighted as any to talk about it. "Well, I don't know. I mean, I'm going through changes about that, you know. I'm delighted about it. I didn't think that I ever would—somewhere inside me, you know, I've always wanted to be a father. I want a little boy. When

186

I say that to Kathleen, she says I'm a male chauvinist. But if it's a little girl, I can dig it. Well, you know I'll be even more responsible, because—you see children are really the people that I dig. . . ."

He told about watching a mother once who never talked to her children. She "always screamed at them and she would treat them as though they were stupid. I looked at her little boy, and the cat was uptight, and he was like *enraged*, and I wondered what was wrong with him, you know? I observed the situation, and it occurred to me that it was just because no one talked to him, that he was being treated as though he couldn't think or that he wasn't a sensible person, and that they seemed to be waiting for him to get older, and then he would start thinking. So I started talking to him. And it was very clear to me that you could hold an intelligent conversation with the child. I brought this to her attention and I made her start talking to the cat, you know, and he just changed, because he was being communicated with. Even though he couldn't really talk good, he could communicate."

I don't know whether the implication in that anecdote escaped Lockwood or not. He didn't comment on it. But I think there is considerable insight into Eldridge right here—maybe a considerable part of the basis of his racial-revolutionary struggle. Is rage the result of someone sensing or feeling or thinking that someone else thinks he or she is too stupid or not worth communicating with? Can you boil revolution down to these human terms? Wasn't that the basis of all of Eldridge's inflammatory rhetoric?

Lockwood made no analysis. But the interview ended with his asking Eldridge what he felt his biggest failings were, what he had to work hardest to overcome. With humor and typical honesty, Eldridge replied "Talking too much. I think that's my biggest problem. I'm a fat mouth and a fool, you know? I talk too much."

I'm sure the little boy he talked to didn't mind at all.

* * * *

Apart from admitting he was a sucker for kids, Eldridge sounded harder than ever, colder, more on ice than ever. Whatever happened to that thaw I thought I detected back there as he hunched over his typewriter in Folsom typing out the bits and pieces of his book? Well, more than one spring thaw has been thwarted by a freezing change in the weather. The temperature of Eldridge's times changed after his parole. He couldn't control the climate, so he became part of it.

And when he left the U.S. he took his times with him, moving into the bigger world where he found the climate similar. So the struggle accompanied Eldridge throughout his exile.

Whatever time he had spent thinking during the early enforced idleness in Cuba had not apparently been in any personal vein, except as he related to the struggle in which he found himself involved. But amidst all that hardness can be seen the idealist Eldridge was at heart, and how deeply American he was. He wouldn't have put it in so many terms, then, but he was to become *proud* to be an American. In 1969 he was in the homeland of the Algerian psychiatrist Frantz Fanon whose *Wretched of the Earth* legitimized violence in the black struggle by explaining in detail the feelings of oppressed peoples against their masters and noting that part of the liberation process is the resorting to revolutionary violence. Instead of a black—or any oppressed person—feeling guilty for his feelings of hatred over having someone's boot on his neck, he should consider it justifiable to use force to remove the boot because it was taking force to keep the boot on his neck in the first place. Fanon was one of Eldridge's heroes. Along with Castro (somewhat subdued now) and Che Guevara, Marx, Lenin, Mao Tse-tung, Ho Chi Minh, Jomo Kenyatta during his Mau Mau days; and back in Babylon, Malcolm X, Huey Newton and Bobby Seale.

His greatest heroes were Malcolm X and Newton. Eldridge idolized Huey. "I've never known anyone like Huey. . . . I used to say that Huey is some type of mutation. . . ." The key to Newton, Eldridge felt, was "the courage to kill," meaning more ". . . the exceptional quality related to a man who is in misery . . . because of the condition of his people, a man who is unable to be comfortable, unable to adjust to the oppression that his people are subjected to, a man who is forced. . . ."

Bobby Seale in his autobiography, *Seize The Time*, said Eldridge used to say that ". . . Huey P. Newton followed Malcolm X like Jesus Christ followed John the Baptist."

Eldridge would change that view in his Algerian exile, also.

* * * *

That was his starting point, then, in mid-1969. A

committed revolutionary, broadening his horizons beyond the American black struggle, in the center of the Third World network, studying (he had been reading a lot since leaving the U.S., he told Lockwood, and rereading a lot of his old heroes' works) how to make the revolution work in the U.S., what to make of the U.S. in the revolution's aftermath, and how to work out the mechanics of changing and strengthening the Black Panthers from this new world headquarters in Algiers. If there had been a lull in Cuba in which despondency had set in, that had changed. Eldridge was planning and plotting now. He was back in action!

He was also at that other starting point: fatherhood. Kathleen gave birth to a boy, Antonio Maceo, in July, 1969. Eldridge reacted with all the characteristics of a first-time-around father. In the framework of his thinking those days he referred to his infant son as ". . . a real Panther."

* * * *

Eldridge made inroads to improving the family's status by using the Vietnamese as a channel to the representative of the National Liberation Front (NLF). He managed to get to the NLF representative the same day the man was meeting with Algerian President Houari Boumedienne and was promised that the NLF would ask the Algerians to extend to Eldridge all the rights normally given to an important liberation front asking for recognition. Algeria was then the center for the world's liberation movements and the NLF was the most important. So with that, and the contact he had with the Pan-African Conference upcoming, family conditions improved rather quickly.

His new contacts and official recognition apparently sent him traveling quickly, also. A *Time* correspondent met Eldridge in the lobby of the Rossiya Hotel near Red Square in Moscow in October, 1969, "the face still hard and menacing, the bearing still rigid . . ." with Eldridge again wearing a black jacket and still having a little gold button in one earlobe. They talked in a quiet spot on the hotel's seventh floor.

Eldridge told *Time's* correspondent he was "very happy" in Algeria, that he was able to move "virtually at will in Communist countries, using nothing but his California driver's license and an FBI wanted poster in lieu of a passport." He was critical of the Soviet Union's backing down from confrontations with the United States more than once, and showed new affection for North Korea's Premier Kim I Sung who had stepped into the vacuum created in the international proletarian movement by the squabbling Soviets and Red China.

He was as "involved as ever in the United States," and fully intended "to keep functioning against the oppressive system there. . . . It's important for people to fight in the terrain they know best. Being in exile is not my bag at all."

He expected revolution to come in his lifetime, with the Panthers in the vanguard.

By December he was so "involved" in U.S. affairs that when Panthers were slain in a shoot-out with Chicago police, he and three alleged hijackers, according to an Associated Press story, showed up at a U.S. diplomatic office in Algiers asking for passports to return home. When told they could get only a certificate of identity good for a one-way trip to the

U.S., the four left and did not return.

* * * *

Around the end of 1969-70 Gordon Parks of *Life* found Eldridge "outside of Algiers in one of those yellowish-white concrete houses that line the Mediterranean coast . . . slumped in a chair, his legs stretched out, the infant (Antonio Maceo) slung across his shoulder. He gently massaged the baby's back. . . ." Displayed prominently on one wall was a large poster photo of Huey Newton.

Parks had a lot of questions. Did Eldridge plan to return to the U.S.? What did he think about all the Panther gun battles with police back home? And questions about "the struggle" in general.

Yes, Eldridge would return. "I'm going back home to San Francisco." Eldridge gave his old Pine Street address. "Nobody is going to keep me away from it."

About the gunfights: "Crap . . . So we have to be shot up and murdered in our homes before people become indignant . . . What are we supposed to do, pray for deliverance? . . . . The cops who murdered (Panther members) must be punished in the same way they committed the crime."

The situation back home was worse for the Panthers and the police. All year long both sides had suffered woundings and deaths. The Panthers were claiming twenty eight members killed by police. Of nineteen photos of dead Panthers in Parks' *Life* article February 6, 1970, ten had been ruled "justifiable homicide." Three of the killings had been in 1968, all the others in 1969.

Parks asked about rumors that the Black Panthers were being infiltrated by Communists.

"Black people don't need Communists to teach them about trouble," Eldridge replied. "The jails in Babylon produce more rebels and revolutionaries than the Communists could dream of producing. . . ."

Over lamb stew that Kathleen brought in they talked about the revolution, the guerrilla warfare to come. "What will you build from the rubble?" Parks asked.

"Social justice," Eldridge replied.

Parks thought of Malcolm X and Martin Luther King, and felt that Eldridge's promise, like theirs, "would go unfulfilled. Social justice, it seems, is much more difficult to come by than martyrdom," Parks wrote.

Eldridge asked Parks if he'd like to join the party. Parks said no; if he were younger, yes (he was fifty-seven); besides Parks had things to write about the struggle. Wouldn't Eldridge be better off, too, writing from Algiers than returning home?

"You can't fight pigs with eloquence. I've got to physically commit myself," Eldridge answered.

Parks wrote in his *Life* article, "If he comes back, I believe it is to avoid another kind of death. The death inside him in exile is as bad as the other kind of death I fear awaits him" back in the states. "Cleaver is armored with the brutal truth of Panther history, of hard streets and tough prisons. Yet a basic naivete makes him vulnerable at times."

I wonder, how much was exile eating away inside Eldridge despite all his outward international activity?

* * * *

1970 was a year of ups and downs for Eldridge and his revolutionary relatives. Back home in the States, everything was down: twenty-eight Black Panther Party members killed allegedly by concerted police efforts; Huey Newton in prison for manslaughter; Bobby Seale jailed in Chicago, held under $25,000 bail on charges of murdering another Panther in Connecticut, as well as being on trial in Chicago with seven others for the 1968 Democratic National Convention fracas; David Hilliard, the party chief, out on bail pending trial for threatening the life of President Nixon. Vice President Spiro Agnew was calling the Panthers "a completely irresponsible, anarchistic group of criminals"; the U.S. Attorney General's office was calling them "hoodlums"; FBI Director J. Edgar Hoover was to call them the "biggest single threat to the country's internal security."

There were other lesser things, too. Stories were appearing in January that Kathleen was in Paris, en route back to the U.S. and that Eldridge himself "might try to slip back . . . within the next few days." (That last came from the Panther newspaper, which said Kathleen and the boy would visit her parents in Washington, D.C., and that Eldridge would return the way he left and "start working to help Negroes take our freedom.") Another wire story said Kathleen planned to make Paris her home "indefinitely."

In March the San Francisco Bay Area papers reported that a deadlocked jury had resulted in a mistrial for two Panther members tried for the April 6, 1968 shoot-out; two others were already in prison for that, sentenced to up to fifteen years; trials for four others were pending; Eldridge was still in exile in

Algiers.

In Algiers, though, things were looking up for the Cleavers. The United Press relayed a CBS story that the Arabs were "establishing close ties of solidarity" with the Panthers there and were discussing possibilities of training Panther members in guerrilla warfare tactics. Some had reportedly already taken part in Arab operations in the Middle East.

Bigger things than this were happening. In late summer Eldridge and Kathleen joined a number of other Americans as members of the "United States Peoples' Anti-Imperialist Delegation" to visit Asian Communist capitals. The *New York Times* said Eldridge called it 'a tour of solidarity' to 'cement political alliances' with Asian revolutionary forces." The group visited Peking, Hanoi and Pyongyang and even staged a demonstration before American military police at Panmunjom in the demilitarized zone of Korea.

Most important, on their return, the Black Panthers opened up a swank international headquarters in a handsome three-story white villa in the El Biar suburban heights section of Algiers. The grand opening reception was attended by ranking members of African and Asian embassies and top Algerian officials. The affair was far better than a "coming out party"; for Eldridge it was a "finally in party," the public formal indication that the Algerians had accorded the Panthers official status as a "liberation movement." As if to punctuate this with absolute assurance, on the columns of the entrance gate were two shining brass plaques showing a crouching panther bearing the designation: "Black Panther Party—International

Section."

Eldridge, with justifiable elation, was as eloquent and dramatic as ever in his announcement of the achievement: "This is the first time in the struggle of the black people in America that they have established representation abroad."

The new headquarters would provide a haven for black American exiles, and would function as a close liaison with other liberation movements. Eldridge said he learned many things on his Asian trip. He found black GI deserters in Europe, and black U.S. deserters fighting with the Vietcong; through the new headquarters he would be involved in recruiting as many of those as possible.

"Of course, it's frustrating," the *New York Times* quoted him in an insert in Sanche de Gramont's story in the November 1st edition of the *Magazine*, "to live in exile. I'd much prefer to be there (in the United States). . . . All I do is toward the idea of going back, but not to surrender myself to those pigs. . . . I find it impossible to relate to the judicial system in the U.S. . . .

"Here in Algiers . . . through this technique (of the International Section), we internationalize our struggle, we show that oppression is an international problem. . . . We are going to bring up the issue . . . in the International public forum. . . . Although we realize that the United Nations is only a puppet of the United States, we are going to lay a concrete proposal before the U.N. . . . We are a liberation movement in every sense of the word."

He cited the heavy losses the party had suffered in police battles in the U.S., but declared that

". . . repression strengthens our party," and that there were "underground aspects . . . Panther members no one knows about." And he drew attention to the singular feature of the American struggle—that it was an urban revolution, and thus different from the world's other revolutionary movements which had been, and were being, fought in rural areas and jungles. And always, the reminder: "My ambition is the destruction of the present system. . . ."

However, the crowning achievement was the image the Panthers gained by their new status, contrasted with the official U.S. image in the Third World. In their new headquarters they were the only Americans recognized by the Algerians, de Gramont pointed out in the *New York Times Magazine*. Algeria had broken off diplomatic relations with the U.S. several years before.

In the months to come this would almost lampoon U.S. diplomatic status in the Third World regions. Many times countries not recognizing the U.S. diplomatically would invite Eldridge as the U.S. representative to some conference. Other times both Eldridge and a U.S. official would sit opposite one another at some conference table. In front of them would be their respective plaques. Eldridge's would read: "Black Panther Party," a deep embarrassment to U.S. diplomats who had to share equal recognition with a man who was on the FBI's "Wanted" list.

Another aspect of September, 1970, was not so bright. It started out bright enough, but ended in disarray and near disaster. Dr. Timothy Leary, notorious czar of LSD and acid trips, and his wife Rosemary sought asylum in Algiers. At first Eldridge thought it a good idea to sponsor him. He thought

Leary might somehow add to the party's status.

Realizing that the doctor was educated only in his own tripping and not in the revolutionary cause, Eldridge even went so far as to "politicalize" him and help him write a prospectus of why he wanted asylum—a requirement of the Algerian government. The Algerians were somewhat skeptical of Leary, whom they called the "Pope of Dope," but their minds were changed by Eldridge's persuasion and by the immense amount of publicity arising from Eldridge's plans to have Leary and a "Miss Dohrn" at a news conference together. Eldridge admitted later he ripped off the press on the "Miss Dohrn" bit. Everyone thought it was the famed Bernardine, but it was really her sister Jennifer.

At any rate, Leary and Rosemary began to cause all sorts of problems. Eldridge found out that Leary was passing out acid to everyone who sought it, and even trying to sell his solution for all problems to newcomers. Moreover, Leary and his wife would drop acid between themselves, then go out in the desert to trip out, lying naked in the sands. They were discovered by a shepherd once and turned over to the authorities who immediately asked Eldridge a lot of questions.

It so happened that Eldridge also found out about some kid who had sneaked ten thousand acid tabs into the country inside his stereo. Leary stashed the stuff in his apartment until Eldridge found out and demanded that Leary turn it all over to him. When Leary and his wife were turned in to the authorities for the desert-tripping, Eldridge figured the doctor was bad news and told of the ten thousand acid tabs he'd taken from Leary. When the Algerians didn't believe the wild tale, Eldridge went home, got the tabs and offered them as evidence. He had had enough of Leary, and canceled the press conference. He "busted Leary," he told Rolling Stone free-lancer Curtice Taylor a year or so later. The press made a big to-do about Leary's disappearance, accusing the Panthers of kidnapping him. The whole affair sent shadows over the Panther headquarters.

* * * *

The incredible ups and downs continued into 1971, when there developed a split in the Panther party between Eldridge and those at home. Home folks called Eldridge's operation too far-out, too revolutionary; at the time the Panthers had pulled in their old aggressive horns and were into community work on a big scale. By 1971 affection between Eldridge and Huey Newton was gone. Panther ranks split wide open. In February, an astounding conflict burst into the open between Newton (now out of prison after his manslaughter conviction had been overturned by the Court of Appeals) and Eldridge on Jim Dunbar's televised talk show in San Francisco. The two Panther leader-friends brought their disaffection before the world via a long-distance telephone conversation San Francisco-Algiers. Telling about it to *Playboy* in 1973, Newton said Cleaver opened that conversation with "Hi, I'm splitting the party down the middle."

In March, 1971, newspapers carried the story of Eldridge's announcement that he was expelling Newton and David Hilliard, acting party chief in the

States, from the Panthers. Simultaneously the Black Panther Party newspaper ran a big story about Eldridge holding Kathleen "prisoner" in the Algiers villa.

The party fight went on all year. By October, Kathleen, on a visit to the U.S., told a news conference, "The Black Panther Party is dead," declaring that while in prison Newton had been tampered with through the use of drugs and brainwashing and physical force so that on his release he had gone out and caused the party's difficulties.

By the 1973 *Playboy* interview Newton was declaring even worse things about Eldridge, saying that Eldridge had been responsible for the excessive display of guns by the Panthers in the old days, that his rhetoric had far exceeded the party's actual activities, and that it was Eldridge's idea to use obscene language so excessively in all his oratory. Newton even went so far as to imply that Eldridge's criticism that black author James Baldwin's admitted homosexuality weakened the black cause stemmed from the fact that Eldridge himself was a repressed homosexual.

The party split was irreconcilable. Eldridge Cleaver became anathema to Newton, Hilliard, Seale and the home country Panthers, who ended by expelling him; they in turn became a lost cause, and Huey a fallen hero, to Eldridge. The split also had a strong effect on the Algerians. The downtrend continued throughout 1972, with the Algerians frowning more deeply as time passed, on the Panther presence within their borders. So, by late March, 1973, the *New York Times* released a story nationwide which was headlined in the *San Francisco Chronicle* on the 29th: "The Black Panthers

Have Vanished From Algeria."

The handsome villa in the El Biar section of Algiers, "is shut and closed. No one answers the bell. All the shutters are closed and the brass plaques are dirty. Neighbors . . . say that all the Panthers left about three weeks ago, taking their possessions with them. They have apparently departed the country. . . .

"Last August 10 (1972) the Panther headquarters . . . was raided by Algerian police. . . ." One leader had left in September without notice, and shortly after, Donald Cox, a longtime associate of Eldridge, ". . . published an open letter dissociating himself from all Panther activities. Cox has not been seen in Algeria since December. Cleaver has not been seen since January."

While not giving their reasons for leaving Algiers, a story in the San Francisco *Jewish Bulletin*, June 4, 1976, from a speech by Kathleen to a Jewish group and from an interview with her, gave Cleaver-side insights as to their growing dissatisfaction with life in the Third World back in 1970-73.

In earlier days the Panthers had been critical of the Zionist movement, and at that time the Jews in the Bay Area looked with fear on the Panthers. Eldridge had raised questions about the Panthers' views, but had never been able to get a real handle on the Arab-Jewish situation in the Middle East. He once said that when he asked he could not get good answers about it from Jewish people. Lucid about everything else ". . . they would become vague and elusive," he said.

Finally the wife of Mario Savio (head of the Berkeley Free Speech Movement) told Eldridge she supported Israel. "She was the first Jew in the [Black] Movement to say it. It made a great impression on me," Eldridge declared.

When he got to Algiers he began to see for himself many of the very kinds of things he was so rabidly opposed to. Black slaves in Arab homes. Scornful attitudes from strangers. "They would call you *kulasha* which meant 'slave.' " Eldridge found racism rampant throughout the Third World—in Egypt, Tunisia, Sudan and Libya as well as Algiers. "Blacks were given room and board and were responsible for all their 'owners' needs; they were called 'Nubians.' " Visiting a prospective landlord while apartment hunting in Algiers, he saw the woman waited on by a black woman, "barefooted, with gold bracelets around her wrists and ankles," whom the landlady said had been given to her as a present when she (the landlady) had had children. "The dream life for Arabs was a villa, a Citroen auto, and a slave," said Eldridge. He came to the conclusion that support for Arabs among black Americans was "knee-jerk traditional skin-game politics," aided by Arab investment in black enterprises.

* * * *

So with affection and support disintegrating on all sides, the grand scheme of revolution to bring about not only black liberation but liberation for all oppressed peoples fell in shambles. Time in another world, the Third World, had run out. The Cleavers, as well as all the other Panthers, vanished from Algeria. Exile for Eldridge and Kathleen and their children (daughter Joju had been born in North Korea) became now a dreary hidden pilgrimage.

CHAPTER THREE

FRANCE

1975. For months the international press wires had been silent about the Cleavers. Once in a while, a reference to Eldridge appeared in some story about the now milder Panthers. On March 12th, a United Press dispatch published in the Berkeley, California *Gazette*, about old Panther leaders who had gone on, contained an interesting sentence: "One lives in exile in Paris and the whereabouts unknown."

Eldridge wasn't in hiding, so reporters did manage to find him from time to time. Free-lance photographer-writer Curtice Taylor, whose father Frank Taylor had been the McGraw-Hill editor who brought out *Soul on Ice*, ran across Eldridge in September, 1974, and the two had talked in a Paris cafe. Eldridge frankly admitted he was homesick. But Taylor's long, in-depth article would not appear in *Rolling Stone* until September, 1975.

So if it hadn't been for *Newsweek*'s updated profile by Jane Friedman in the March 17, 1975, issue, Eldridge would still have remained little more than a memory of times past. Finding him an "old Panther with a new purr," Miss Friedman filled in the missing years. They were tinged with sadness. Eldridge had changed vastly.

"After six years of exile," Miss Friedman cabled, "he seems a softer, mellower man. His beard is gone and so is the fierceness in his hazel eyes. His close-cropped hair is full of gray strands that betray his 39 years, and the leather outfits of his Panther years have been replaced by turtlenecks and cheap pants."

Eldridge's rhetoric wore different apparel, too. The militancy was gone, she noted, and "he no longer wants to bring down the American system. He wants to come home and live with it.

". . . He now says that exile has been another form of prison. . . .

"Since leaving Algeria . . . after a hassle . . . two years ago . . . Cleaver has fallen on hard times. He lives now with his wife Kathleen, and two children, Maceo and Joju, in a small house in a working-class district of Paris. The walls are papered and the floor strewn with memorabilia of his Panther days: newspaper clippings, photos of himself and his wife and black notables like Dr. Martin Luther King, Jr. and Malcolm X, a pair of worn black combat boots, bookcases full of tapes and stacks of papers that he says are notes for a new book, *Over My Shoulder*. His prize possession is a shortwave radio he uses daily to tune in news from America. 'If it came down to a choice between a woman and a radio,' Cleaver remarked, 'I'd choose the radio. It brings the outside world in.' "

His views had been re-outfitted, also. He had "cooled on Communism as a result of his visits to China, Russia and several European countries. Cleaver has concluded that the Marxist world view is 'static' and no longer relevant to modern societies." He felt the Russians were capable of launching a surprise attack and that America needed a strong defense establishment. A "cultural chasm" had separated him from the Third World, and he told Miss Friedman, "I felt as distant from the Africans as I did from the Asians."

As for America, the wrenching moral scandal of Watergate " 'changed everything,' he said. 'It was America's greatest contribution.' He is optimistic about the nation and its possibility of change. Because of the scandal and the fall of President Nixon, many of the ideas of the left have come to be accepted." Reform hadn't gone far enough, though, and he was still saying that the U.S. "should concentrate on applying the universal principles of socialism to our history, our situation and our needs."

Buried among the quotes was the striking comment that he favored "closely controlled police forces to guarantee public safety." Only a full page of exclamation points could accentuate that remark strongly enough. Had time run out also on his hatred of the pigs?

Apparently. The Panther party "is a closed chapter and so is political violence," although Eldridge felt that others would continue to use it. His ambition in March, 1975, was to settle in California where people have room to be 'human' and become a sort of armchair philosopher for the left. 'Somehow man is less grand than I would have thought,' he ruminates. 'He's okay, but he's less grand.' "

Miss Friedman reported that Eldridge was "living

hand to mouth because the U.S. treasury has blocked royalties—running to six figures—from his book. . . ." Viking Press had given him $40,000 in advance over the past three years on his next book, before he canceled the contract and agreed to repay the sum. That the U.S. was still blocking royalties from *Soul on Ice* came as a surprise, because although Lee Lockwood had pointed out in 1969 that the government had stopped Eldridge from receiving them because he had become a "Cuban national" under an obscure law, other writers later said he had been reinstated and was getting the money.

And then *Newsweek* printed Eldridge's everlasting admission: Yes, he was willing to stand trial for the April 6, 1968 shootout, but he didn't want to be slapped back in prison on the old parole revocation while waiting for the trial to begin and end. He had said that all during the days before he had slipped into exile in 1968. That much of Eldridge hadn't changed.

* * * *

Newsweek's Miss Friedman had unearthed Eldridge Cleaver, and dusted him off for the world to look at once again. It was a good story, but she didn't know the story she had *almost* uncovered in this last wilderness of Eldridge's long exile. She had only peeped through the blinds that shut out all that the years had done to him.

It wasn't poor reporting. Miss Friedman couldn't possibly have gotten the whole story. Eldridge couldn't have explained it to her then; he didn't know it all himself. The long-delayed ice jam was finallly breaking up. The inner thaw which had appeared so long ago back in that private cell on the honor block at Folsom Prison but which the climate of the times had refrozen so solidly, was spreading. Miss Friedman just walked across chunks of ice melting in the warming current.

The story of what the Cleavers were going through at this time wasn't to come out until months later, when, after his exile, Eldridge himself understood it all and began to explain it.

* * * *

It had been tricky, vanishing from Algiers. Everything had come down in the Third World just as it had back in the U.S. and then in Cuba. The Cleavers had to get out, but where were they to go? For years in Algiers Eldridge had manufactured forged passports for Algerian students wanting to get to France. So now, why not one for himself? He didn't have to worry about Kathleen and the children. They weren't fugitives. So he forged a passport, kissed the Third World goodbye and headed for France.

At first it appeared that France wouldn't be a haven after all. Officials there knew of him and had doubts of why he wanted asylum in their country. They finally relented and accepted him on the grounds that he absolutely shun all political activity. He agreed. The family set up housekeeping in Paris, and Eldridge set up a "work apartment" in Rocheville in southern France on the fringes of the French Riviera.

Here he kept all his books, his manuscripts, his typewriter, accouterments of revolutionary days, mementoes of the struggle. For a man like Eldridge, with the never-satiated demand for privacy, the twelfth-floor apartment with a balcony view of the Mediterranean was an exquisite sanctuary. It was a place to think, to pick up the search he had abandoned long ago in the press of the liberation turmoil. A place to work on another book instead of Black Panther communiques. Also a place in which to melt. And a place for a spiritual French Connection.

Asylum in France proved unsatisfying. Eldridge arrived from Algiers in a state of turmoil. The philosophies and ideologies he had so given himself to were unable to answer the problems troubling him. He was down on dictatorships, the Communist Party, military governments. Throughout his travels in socialist countries and the Third World he had come to understand that if he wanted to do anything good to them, he had better support the *people* in those countries rather than the Boumediennes, the Brezhnevs, the Castros, or the Mao Tse-tungs of the world. Regardless of how good those people were in their hearts, or how much good they had done for their people, or how much good they wanted to do, everything was negated by the yoke of dictatorship they had placed on the necks of their peoples. None of any of it was any longer something he could support or enjoy.

All his philosophies and ideologies were falling apart, and they weren't being replaced by anything. He was feeling more uptight and useless. Inwardly he felt rotten, corrupt and doomed—completely at a dead end. Because of his heroes, Castro, Guevara, Fanon, Marx, Newton, what had he become? Freedom fighter, revolutionary, spokesman, erstwhile diplomat in

Algiers vamping on the legitmate U.S. representatives, pilgrim, wanderer from country to country, unwelcome in nation after nation. And now the last hero—himself—was going the way of all the others. He didn't even respect himself any more. That was the bottom line he kept coming back to in the enveloping dismay.

Some place along the line, although Eldridge has not to my knowledge expressed it publicly in these terms, he began to tie together the linkage of himself as a human to his heritage that extended all the way back to Eden. His children were the first link. In Maceo and him into contact with the chain of life. In Maceo and Joju Eldridge saw in miniature his eyes and his ears and his nose. And he thought back to his mother and father and how they had passed their life on to him. Not only had they passed it on to him, but in a young form, reborn, and each time there had been a gain involved.

Nowhere in Marxism, Leninism, or historical materialism was this dealt with. Their philosophy couldn't deal with this chain of life which Eldridge saw in his children. Marx and Lenin had no place for the soul. They couldn't deal with man's spirit. In fact, he thought, they had trouble even dealing with electricity because it behaved in some strange way inconsistent with their theories.

In everything he had believed in his life, up to these months in France, something was missing.

"At the end of the line," he would tell audiences later, "after all my travels all over the world, I realized that what was missing in my life . . . was God. . . . There's something involved that is worthy of being called God because it is worthy of respect."

Recognition of that missing element caught him by surprise, shook him. The thought sneaked in quietly at first and sat down unobtrusively in a corner of his mind to wait for recognition. Eldridge had reached a dead end, but he had to pound on it for a while before he fully realized how dead it was. God could wait; He has supreme, everlasting patience.

The days and months stretched into a year, then two. As he told *Newsweek*, exile was just another form of prison. France became a kind of solitary confinement. Eldridge would spend as much time as he could, a week, maybe two or three, in southern France, until he couldn't stand being away from Kathleen and the children any longer, then he would hop a plane for Paris for a few days. Then back to Rocheville. Then return to Paris. He became a commuter in this last prison of exile—a kind of pacing back and forth from one wall of the territorial cell to the other.

He kept watching his children growing up in French schools. They were learning to speak French, with Maceo coming home and not wanting to speak English. The two were becoming little French children. Not that Eldridge had anything against the French people; they were very nice and hospitable, but he didn't want his children to become French. They were Americans. Kathleen was American. Eldridge was American. The children's heritage was American, but so far America had not become their birthright. Maceo had been born in Algeria; Joju in North Korea. They were exiles, like their parents—like their father, mostly, because Eldridge had gotten his family into all this.

That thought particularly ate at him. He had always been difficult to live with. Now he began giving

Kathleen a hard time, almost as though he were intentionally trying to drive her away from him. Subconsciously at first, and later more consciously, that was exactly what he was trying to do. She and the children could go back home. Let him stay here. They didn't have to suffer his exile with him. But Kathleen, statuesque as ever even in the small Parisian apartment, was as dogmatic as he was. She wouldn't go. She never once criticized him, accused him, blamed him for what he had brought on them all. She stayed and took it and that was that. And that loyalty knifed through him along with all the other realizations.

He kept trying to find ways to solve his dilemma. Listening to and watching what was going on back in America, with Watergate, with Vice President Agnew's shameful departure then President Nixon's more astounding resignation and Attorney General John Mitchell's indictment, Eldridge keened to the startling changes his homeland was encountering. He even began to experience the strange feeling of excitement and thrill.

"One of the greatest moments that I experienced in all the time I was abroad," he was to admit later, "was at the time of the Watergate hearings, and the desperate efforts to terminate the war in Indochina, and the very complicated negotiations around the world. . . .

"With all of those things going on, it was thrilling to see the relentless process of housecleaning going on, with nothing being swept under the rug. All that unraveling of the cover-up. The greatest political education in the history of the world was taking place. It was fascinating to me to see how other people around the world were reacting. . . .

"Governments like the Soviet Union, Egypt and France—still a democracy but where there is a log of the divine right of kings still present—all those governments became terrified by the process going on in America, because it was being said by the process that no man, including even the president of a country, was above the law.

"This had people around the world shaking. Leaders were worried because they were taking a closer look at their own governments and they were finding that there was a lot of work yet to be done. It made me feel good. I experienced the real, warm renewal of faith and trust in the machinery of the American government. . . ."

An unexplainable nostalgia filtered through him as he saw the U.S. dealing with all of its internal problems, the war, the diplomacy by people who were trying to take the opportunity of difficulties at home and abroad to advance their own private causes. Observing it all, he saw that, far from being unable to deal with all those problems, the very openness with which the whole housecleaning process was taking place was a source of tremendous national strength.

". . . It was beautiful to watch the regeneration going on in broad daylight for the whole world to see. . . ."

The growing excitement was heightened by the news that a lot of his old friends were making it into high political offices. Ron Dellums moved into a California congressional seat. Mervyn Dymally became the state's lieutenant governor. His old enemy Ronald Reagan was replaced by a new man, Edmund Brown, Jr. who, although he went a little far out with his meditative practices, at least *concentrated* on problems.

And Eldridge also saw a lot of other blacks moving into elected offices around the country. Even an old police lieutenant friend whom Eldridge had known from his Los Angeles days was now mayor there. Blacks were becoming more active in police departments and legislatures around the country. If the times had changed downward for Eldridge, they were certainly on the upswing at home. It gave him new hope.

Maybe *my* time has come, he thought. Maybe *I* can go back now and get a fair trial in this new climate.

That thought became the chorus of a new song in his life. He repeated it over and over as he began to contact those old friends who had new political power. "Hey, look," he told them. "Help me come back home. I want to come back to the States. It ought to be possible. Why you're even talking about the possibility of a black man becoming president. Surely I ought to be able to come back now. I'm willing to stand trial."

Nobody else sang along with him.

In the changing American times, the Black Panther Party had undergone drastic cosmetic surgery. As the *Berkeley Gazette* said in March, 1975, ". . . The dominant public figure of the Black Panthers is a winsome thirty-two-year-old former school teacher, Elaine Brown. She has the Black Panthers giving free breakfasts to children and free transportation to the elderly. . . . Mrs. Brown currently is running for a seat on the Oakland City Council. She campaigns with the air of a gracious suburban housewife, and has endorsements from several Democratic clubs and AFL-CIO groups. . . ."

But the old friends whom Eldridge called still heard the distant echoes of police gunfire against Panther members and the vitriolic exchange of Huey Newton's and Eldridge's internecine party warfare. The "old friends"—they were dissipating so that they had to be referred to in quotes now—didn't want to get involved in any fight between Eldridge and Huey. It didn't make any difference that the old guard had long since vanished: Newton, in jail and out on repeated trials and then finally involved in another fracas which made another trial necessary, had finally jumped $42,000 bail in 1974 and was reportedly in Havana (following Eldridge's exile footsteps?); Bobby Seale who had come out of all his court trials to campaign unsuccessfully for the office of mayor of Oakland in 1973, had disappeared. He was reported at one time to be recuperating from an illness and finally to be seeking a job in his old profession as a comedian, hoping for a job in the movies.

The "old friends" turned thumbs down on Eldridge. Comfortably ensconced in the new American political structure, they had severed all their old ties. The warming thrill Eldridge had felt watching the national housecleaning chilled, left him increasingly despondent. Depression came in like a tide that never ebbed, its waves eroding his inner shoreline.

Things worsened when another old acquaintance visiting in Paris told Eldridge the blunt truth: "You might as well forget it, Eldridge. You got a thick head if you can't understand what's happening. You might as well learn how to speak French and become a black Frenchman, because they're not going to help you come back because they don't want you to come back. There's no place there for you. The whole pecking order has changed and you just don't fit in any more. There's a new thing going on over there, so forget it."

It was as though a ton of bricks had been dropped on him.

Another crushing blow came with the news that his father had died in June, 1975. It was a terrible shock. When his father had been alive Eldridge hadn't really had much contact with him, but when he died—well, it hit Eldridge that never again would he ever have any contact with him. Knowing that your relationship with your father has ended for all time has impact different from anything else in life. Although much remains, something solid is sucked out of you and you're vacant inside. That spot where dad was is empty. And it always will be.

His Paris-Rocheville-Paris commute continued. One night he came into the Paris apartment to find Kathleen preparing dinner. He was turned inside out as they sat down to dinner. To make things cozier, they turned out all the lights and set candles on the table. But instead of warming the family, the candlelight cast shadows. Eldridge looked at Maceo on one side and Joju on the other and Kathleen across from him. He read the same thing in each of their faces, behind their eyes. The kids didn't understand what was happening, but they sensed the gloom. Kathleen's beauty was subdued by the candlelight and shadows rather than enhanced. Eldridge fought inwardly to keep from jumping up and running out of the apartment. He looked around and saw the place was in darkness.

"There were no lights in our house," he would describe later. "There were no goals, no purpose in our lives, no organization to our system. We just sat there like bumps on a log. Kathleen looked so sad. It just wasn't right. Four people lost in the darkness and it was my fault. . . ."

Eldridge conquered his impulse to flee that night, but first thing the next morning he headed for the airport and a plane back to the south of France. That night he went out to sit on the balcony as he did so frequently, to watch the blue-silver waters of the Mediterranean and the opaque depths of the sky. The balcony was a place of peace for him. The stars and the moon, hanging there in the sabled blackness of the sky, had endless enchantment to them. You could look at a star then find yourself looking beyond it into the blackness to another star so that the whole heavens became a platter of jewels in the night.

Still churning inwardly from the previous night, more convinced than ever that the dead end he pounded on was absolutely lifeless, that the future held nothing but futility, Eldridge let his eyes wander over the panoramic sky as thoughts of suicide drifted through his mind. *That* would be a solution. With him out of the way, Kathleen would have no ties binding her to France. She could take the kids and go back home where they all belonged. He toyed with the ominous idea for some time while he watched the shadows shift and reassemble on the face of the moon as it made its nightly pass around the earth.

Shadows. Faces. Man in the moon. Man's footsteps were up there. Idly watching the moon shadows form and reform he suddenly saw his own image take shape. He recognized it instantly—the same profile he had seen a million times on Black Panther posters. He

216

began to get nervous, then frightened as the image hung there on the moon's face. He tried to control a growing apprehension by telling himself he was just tripping out on the moon, but it was impossible to reassure himself. The feeling of dread expanded, intensified; an overwhelming fear was welling up inside. Something terrible or horrible was touching him, like death. That was it—he felt in contact with death itself. He wondered if seeing oneself in the moon was some kind of premonition and wished he knew something about folklore. He began to tremble as the inner fright mounted, and then the trembling got worse, coming from someplace deep inside, shaking his soul. He had been scared before and had trembled before, but never like this. Then his image rolled away, but in its place came a succession of familiar faces—Fidel Castro, Karl Marx, Friedrich Engels, Mao Tse-tung, all his old heroes. What was happening to him, anyway? Was he finally losing his mind as he had lost his life's momentum and purpose?

Then, of all the faces in heaven and earth, the face of Jesus Christ formed out of the moon shadows. Eldridge never thought about Christ. Jesus was the last thing ever to enter his mind—the last person to hold his attention, except briefly when he'd toss Christ in along with all his other revolutionary heroes. He couldn't look away. He just gaped and trembled and shook, and as Christ's face became clearly distinct, everything exploded.

Eldridge came apart in a flood of sobbing tears, crying uncontrollably, unable to stop the terrible inner shaking. He fell out of the chair to his knees and cried until somewhere out of some crevice of memory came

217

the words of the Lord's Prayer, followed by those of the Twenty-third Psalm. He heard the words tumble through his lips. Over and over and over he repeated the words. Each time he said them he could feel the incessant inner shaking subsiding. He felt if he kept saying the words, he could bring himself under control, so he repeated them again and again. "The Lord is my shepherd, I shall not want. . . ." Finally the tremors lessened. Exhausted, he knelt there until he felt strong enough to get up. He went immediately to his bookshelves and took down the copy of the family Bible his mother had given him because he was the oldest son. Funny, if Kathleen hadn't stuffed it into her suitcase, it would still be back in San Francisco. He had asked her why she had brought it with her to Algiers instead of bringing something else and she had just said it seemed the right thing to do so she'd jammed it in the suitcase with all the clothes and other things. He sat down, turned to the Twenty-third Psalm and noticed that he'd been misquoting it. Somewhere down the verses he'd forgotten the words since he'd learned them so long ago. He read them over now, and reread them, and let his eyes drift to other passages. Gradually all the trembling ceased. The words began to swim before his eyes, so he closed the Bible and set it down, made his way to the bedroom and collapsed on the bed. He was asleep in an instant.

Telling people later about that night, Eldridge says, "I tell you I slept the most peaceful sleep I've ever known in my life. I've never slept that way before or since. The next morning I woke up with a start and jumped out of bed full of energy, ready to play football if anyone offered."

He felt *alive*! More alive than in years. The world was amazingly clear, his life stretching before him in a path as straight as an arrow. Almost immediately on awakening the next morning he saw in his mind a shaft of light stretching off into some nether distance, through a dark spot that he recognized immediately as a prison cell. It went in through an opening on one side of that dark cell and out through an opening on the other side. He didn't hear any voices and he wasn't caught up in any vision, but the thought was there, in his mind, clear and concrete as though he could have touched the light beam or rattled the cell bars. He understood the meaning as though someone had explained it all in detail. He had it within his own power to go back home. He didn't have to wait endlessly for any congressman or "old friend" to help him. There *was* a way. And the way was for him to surrender. That dark prison cell meant he'd have to go back to prison. But the light shaft passed on clean through, and he *knew* that after prison everything would be all right. He would come out all right. Jail obviously because he was a fugitive. And the court trial—which he had always said he was willing to stand. And beyond—*Life* was beyond. He didn't need to remain forever a prisoner in exile here on French soil.

He was ready to run to the airport to head back immediately to Paris to tell Kathleen. But something restrained him. He had to let all of last night's incredible happenings settle in on him. He knew he wasn't wrong, that he hadn't been dreaming, that the way home was along that shaft of light—but he had to let it all settle. He wasn't up to doing all that he had planned that day; things were too different, so he canceled everything and used the hours to accommodate himself to all that he had gone through.

A day or two later he felt it was time to tell Kathleen. He had to be about his new plans. He almost blurted the whole thing out to Kathleen on his arrival, but even though he knew she'd grown to expect him to come home and say almost anything under the sun, he had to time this right. Even Kathleen would cock an eye sideways at him if he came right out and started telling her about what he had seen from the balcony.

So he waited until the kids were asleep and he and Kathleen were getting ready for bed. They were sitting on the edge of the bed talking when he told her about the big decision. He skirted around the balcony episode somewhat, but gave her the salient details.

"Honey, I've decided," he said, watching her closely to see how it would come down on her, "we're goin' back home. I'm going to surrender myself, and all this will be over with."

Kathleen's blue eyes lit up and her face burst open with joy. She jumped almost straight up off the bed and went skipping around the bedroom. Her instant, spontaneous reaction signified to Eldridge that he had understood the light shaft and cell thought completely. His decision was the right one—for everybody.

The next day he went into downtown Paris to talk to Samuel Pisar, an attorney he had dealt with before. His request met with surprise from Pisar and the other lawyers there.

"I want you to contact the American authorities and organize my surrender," Eldridge said. "I'm going to give myself up."

The lawyers knew him well, knew he had been

running from the authorities and the police, knew of his prison record, knew how he felt about police and power structures and America. This was strange talk from Eldridge Cleaver.

"Look, Eldridge, is everything all right?" Pisar asked. "Anybody putting any pressure on you?"

"No, no, man. Everything's all right. Just deal with this like I said. Let's get it all together."

Pisar was understandably cautious. "Eldridge, look, why don't you go home and sleep on this and come back tomorrow? If you still feel the same way, we'll move on it. But go back home and think it over. Just to be sure you know what you're doing. Don't jump into this."

Eldridge took the advice. You always have to take a lawyer's advice. They have a way of putting things so that they sound like they're all wisdom. He went home and showed up back at their offices the next day.

"Okay," he said. "Let's move on it. Let's get this over with."

He was anxious to get on with it. Not that he was about to change his mind. It was like standing at the edge of a swimming pool, knowing the water's going to be cold, but knowing also that once you're in, it's great. He knew once he was back home, in the midst of everything, in the dark spot in that shaft of light, he could deal with it. But let's go.

The lawyers nodded. Okay. If that's what you want. One of the attorneys had formerly been a U.S. State Department lawyer and knew Elliot Richardson, then U.S. Ambassador to England. Richardson would know how to proceed. He called and told Richardson that Eldridge Cleaver wanted to surrender, and asked, "How should we go about it?"

Richardson's response was to be the first of a series of skeptical acceptances of Eldridge's intentions: "Well, that'd be a good thing if that's what he wants to do. But how do you know there isn't some kind of trick in it?"

"There's no trick," Eldridge's lawyer said. "He wants to surrender. What kind of a trick is there in that?"

"Well, you know Cleaver. He's always up to something."

Richardson contacted the State Department, and matters worked their way into all the proper channels, with the same question echoing its way across the Atlantic and through Washington. "What's he up to now? You sure there's not some kind of trick in it?"

Official channels were no help to Eldridge's impatience. It boggled his mind to realize that it was so complicated for a fugitive to surrender. It took three weeks before matters were set.

Pisar, in charge of handling all the international legalities, arranged for a press conference on November 17, 1975, the day before Eldridge was finally to return. Eldridge had made arrangements for Kathleen and the children to return separately. He'd been told he'd be going home on the high-security diplomatic flight daily from Paris to New York. Pisar told Eldridge he'd be accompanied by two FBI agents on the trip, but that he wouldn't be under arrest. He couldn't be arrested on French territory, one of the complications that had delayed matters so long. The press conference attracted a crowd, and the news was out. All the growing rumors were correct: Former Black Panther minister of information, federal fugitive for seven years, was voluntarily returning to the United States from his self-imposed exile to give himself up.

The next stop was Kennedy Airport. Date: November 18, 1975.

BOOK FOUR

THE HOMECOMING

CHAPTER ONE

From the moment the Boeing 747 jet lifted off the Paris airport runway, Eldridge felt that TWA Flight 803 was manned totally by FBI agents. From the two companions flanking him to the smiling stewardesses and even the crew up front, he was sure they were all there for one purpose: to see that he wouldn't escape. They all seemed to know one another, called each other by their first names, were too friendly. They were all plants, there to *make sure of him*.

He found some pleasure in the thought. Folks would never get it straight that he was not up to any tricks. He was returning voluntarily to surrender.

Okay, so it was unbelievable. Eldridge Cleaver coming home after seven years of exile, knowing it meant going back into a jail cell? There had to be some slippery strategy behind his move.

There was, but Eldridge couldn't explain *that* to people. How could he expect anyone to understand what had happened to him that night on the balcony in Rocheville? Or to accept his story of the faces in the

227

moon? That was even wilder than his voluntary surrender. No, he had to ride it out this way, letting everyone think what they wanted, do what they wanted. Later for the balcony; later for the moon. It would all come out eventually, after he had let it sift and settle inside first. He couldn't understand it all himself yet, let alone try to explain it to anyone else: even what he had dropped so far to Kathleen hadn't made complete sense, because he knew she didn't really know, didn't really understand what he was saying.

The two agents with him—one white, one black—had met him at the airport, explained again that he wasn't under arrest, that they "could arrest him once the plane entered U.S. air space, but they wouldn't." They would wait until touchdown at Kennedy Airport before going through the official motions, but for all intents and purposes he was in custody right now.

Once airborne, everybody undid their seat belts and settled in for the few hours run over the beclouded Atlantic. From time to time there was conversation, some of it serious, some just pleasant, some even joking about the pickle the FBI was finding itself in with all the current Senate investigations. Why, if things took a strange enough turn, the agents might find themselves cell mates with Eldridge. It was wry, stinging humor, but they accepted the situation equably enough, despite its ironies.

In between talk Eldridge relaxed into his own thoughts, which invariably threaded their way back to the balcony experience. All he knew was that he had made contact with God that night—or maybe it was the other way around. It was a cinch he hadn't gone out there to look at the night sky to hunt for God. He'd gone out there in despair, to clear his head, to mull over suicidal thoughts, to figure some way to end the dismal lives in which he and Kathleen and the kids were trapped. Then God had—what had God done? He didn't know for sure. Broken him? Yes—thrown him to his knees. Convicted him? That, too. Whatever else God had done, He had certainly turned Eldridge around in his shoes. And here he was, homeward bound.

His thinking drifted and circled—private, submerged. He thought, too, about what lay ahead: arrest. The press would be there, a lot of publicity would follow, everybody would wonder. There would be skepticism and suspicion. It was as though he was making two flights home, one public and one private. One the world knew about and the other only he knew about. Maybe someday he could manage to make the two mesh into some cohesive unity, so that everything would make sense. One thing he knew without a shadow of doubt: he had to do what he was doing.

* * * *

Entrance into the invisible boundary of American air space brought brief comment, and then, below, was the American continent. Excitement gutted through Eldridge, visceral and emotional, sparking him to attentiveness. Well, here it comes. I'm back.

Then he was descending from the plane, and someone from the bevy of FBI agents who met him read out the warrant placing him under arrest. It wasn't until he put down his suitcase and put his hands behind his back and felt the cold steel of the handcuffs that he knew his freedom was finally over.

Wow, this was too quick. He began to sweat, wondering for a moment how he was going to deal with this whole thing after all. It didn't occur to him to pray; God hadn't put that in Eldridge's bag yet. Nobody knows the chilling instant of stepping across the boundary line from freedom to handcuffs unless he's gone through it. Steel says it all.

Agent Walter Yees, stern and balding and matching Eldridge in height, walked on Eldridge's left as the FBI cordon closed around and escorted him. They went into the airport building, through customs and the throng of reporters and TV cameramen to the airport's Federal building for fingerprinting and photographing. The press threw questions at him, more than they knew they'd get answers for; Eldridge gave them an answer to the one they asked most often—"I came back because I *wanted* to." A curt reply that offended, but Eldridge wasn't on his own time any more. He belonged to the authorities now.

Newsmen managed to get a few more comments from him in one of the corridors. When they asked about the prospects for his trial on charges of attempted murder in connection with the April, 1968, shoot-out in Oakland, Eldridge answered, "I think a situation now exists in the country where I can have my day in court."

"My day in court." That phrase was to become Eldridge's most repeated assertion in the following months. He would elaborate and explain later, but there was no time that day. Agents processed him through a courtroom in Brooklyn where he was arraigned on charges of unlawful flight to avoid prosecution—a holding charge that was later

230

dismissed—and placed under $100,000 bail. Then he was whisked into a courthouse jail. His first night's sleep in the United States after seven years was on a prison cot. The next morning he was flown to the Federal Corrections Institute in San Diego accompanied by two U.S. Bureau of Prisons marshals.

CHAPTER TWO

The spotlight was on the public Eldridge from the moment of touchdown at Kennedy. The day after his arrival *The New York Times* carried a quote by Black Panther Party spokesman David Dubois letting the world know that, "As far as the party's concerned, he's not going to become a member again under any circumstances." In a second story the *Times* noted that Eldridge had shown reporters the subpoena handed him at the airport signed by Senator James O. Eastland, D-Miss., chairman of the Senate Judiciary Committee ordering him to appear before a subcommittee in January ". . . to testify on terrorist and subversive activities in the United States."

That the repatriated Eldridge Cleaver was going to be phenomenally different from the old Black Panther Cleaver had been telegraphed well ahead. *Newsweek*'s Miss Friedman had described some of the changes back in March. In September, *Rolling Stone* had finally printed the long interview Eldridge had given Curtice Taylor the year before. And on the day Eldridge arrived at Kennedy, *The New York Times* had strategically published an article he had submitted weeks earlier in which he anticipated the kind of questions people would ask. He had pointed out that people were not so interested in *why* he wanted to return as they were in *what* he would do *if allowed* to return. So he detailed once more the whole April 6, 1968 shoot-out, and the injustice in the California Adult Authority's legal irregularities in revoking his parole before he was even tried on the alleged charges from that night. In the same *New York Times* piece he also declared, ". . . the American political system is the freest and most democratic in the world. . . ." and that ". . . we are playing in a brand new ball game."

That kind of talk from this former revolutionary sent a variety of shock waves through widely different quarters. Many who thought of themselves as "we" were outraged.

Nation magazine in its December 6th issue said Eldridge's return ". . . may mark the end of an historical period that began with [Martin Luther] King's assassination," and wondered how the new ball game Eldridge spoke of was really going to be played. *Nation* also picked up the rumors already beginning to circulate, that Eldridge had "made a deal": "He denies he made a deal with anyone regarding his return, but, whatever his motives, as an apostate revolutionary he will be valuable property for the Establishment." The magazine neatly added later that ". . . in the shadows one sees other ex-radicals who decided they liked the American system and its 'basic principles' and cooperated with the Eastlands of the 1950s." But the article did end with the observation that, "as he did in

1968, Cleaver deserves a fair trial and a fair hearing."

The Black Panthers stepped up their criticism. Eldridge stayed in San Diego only over the Christmas holidays and then was moved to Oakland. Shortly after this, Panther chairwoman Elaine Brown labeled Eldridge as "the black community's Patty Hearst," during a press conference. She also accused him of combining "some information with lies to downgrade former comrades." She claimed that Eldridge secretly provided some testimony to Senator Eastland's Judiciary Internal Security Committee, and she counterattacked by telling reporters the party had a secret witness "who heard . . . Cleaver give the orders which resulted in the murder of Black Panther . . . Samuel Napier in New York . . . on April 17, 1971."

Eldridge's lawyer, George V. Higgins of Boston, stoutly denied this, declaring that Kathleen had told the Senate committee that the FBI's COINTELPRO (Counter Intelligence Program) had tried to break up their marriage and actively "attempted to turn the Black Panthers" against Eldridge and ". . . apparently after all this time, they had succeeded."

The damp winter American soil of 1976 hadn't even caked on Eldridge's shoes yet and already he was back in the thick of it. It made good news. Cleaver politics were always startling.

All the reaction wasn't as harsh as the Panthers' obviously; a lot of what appeared to be severe criticism was in another way the healthy skepticism of newsmen who'd been conned by the best over the years and who weren't about to take Eldridge, especially, at face value. People don't make 180-degree turns without good reason, usually for their own benefit. So, what was really in this new Cleaver vocabulary—for himself and everybody else?

So reporters kept close watch on Eldridge at the Federal Corrections Institute in San Diego. They followed him to the Alameda County Jail in Oakland, followed his legal maneuvers through a succession of changing attorneys, checked with the district attorney, got Eldridge himself in jail, and added considerably to the edginess of authorities who detest pre-trial publicity coming from defendants.

As always, Eldridge's laundry all hung out in public to dry. It became obvious that it was cleaner than in the sixties but it still warranted plenty of close inspection, particularly when hints began to appear in early spring, 1976, that Jesus Christ was now part of the former revolutionary's "new repertoire." That kind of news intensified all the public skepticism. It had all the earmarks of another Charles Colson conversion, then top news once more because of Colson's book, *Born Again*, which was making best-seller lists. The secular press now had added reason for skepticism.

However, the "private" Eldridge who made that other trip home was not to be seen quite yet. *That* Eldridge was still putting the pieces of his Mediterranean moon experience together in his soul. He didn't talk about it. For a while longer God put a gag rule on that affair. But even when given the opportunity, the secular press didn't know how at first to deal with this Christian dimension of the new Eldridge; newsfolk kept focusing on his changed political views.

CHAPTER THREE

Of course, Eldridge's political outlook, the expansion of his turnabout thinking, *was* news, particularly since it showed such a resurgence of patriotism and faith in the American system that he had once denounced as the "No. 1 obstacle to human progress." Even religious newspapers, like the biweekly *National Courier*, found his views significant for their readers because Eldridge's thinking went to the human and moral levels of politics. In a long, taped, telephone interview I had with Eldridge from his Oakland jail cell for the *Courier*, he said: ". . . You know, I've seen the civilizations developed under Confucius, under Buddha, under the Hindus, and under Mohammed. And I know myself to be a product of the Christian-Judaeo tradition. . . . After interacting with people of other cultures, it made me more aware of who and what I am. . . . It's like—I'm not in a hallelujah or a fundamentalist kind of bag, but I recognize Jesus and His teachings as being the essential vehicle for that morality that we must have. . . ."

He said that his exile experiences had made him realize that the former Black Panther movement was ". . . very heavily political, very heavy on economic analysis, but it lacked the cohesion that would have come from the content of morality that you find in religion. And I recognize the tragic consequences because that was missing. . . ."

The integration—segregation issue was as vital for the *Courier*'s Christian audience as it was for the secular public. "I think that the tensions of the times," Eldridge continued, "the struggle between integration and separation create a situation where [the] ideal black man or black woman" should contain views embodied in both Martin Luther King, Jr. and Malcolm X. Because of the sixties' violence and the new climate of the United States in 1976, he said, "I feel . . . that the question . . . has been solved for all history as far as black people are concerned. And it's solved in terms of black people now realizing and accepting that they are Americans and that they are here to stay.

"And this is something I want to get across: that we have no home in Africa. And we must realize that we are full members of this organization called the United States of America, and we must press for our full rights here, and stop this fence straddling between should I stay or should I go."

The secular press was beginning to get to the man beneath the political theorist and social critic, too. Also in May, 1976, Jack Slater wrote in *The Los Angeles Times* that the time of ". . . rage is gone," and that Eldridge admitted ". . . I can look back now and say I was naive. Now I don't even like to see myself as an Afro-American. I'm just an American." And Slater heard Eldridge "apologize to Martin Luther King on some points. I now appreciate his awareness, that the basic relationship between communities of people has to be one of love." As to all the skepticism about his drastic turnabout and the accusations from groups like the Panthers, Eldridge answered Slater's question about his chances of survival with ". . . I have no way of rating [my chances], although I do believe that survival can be organized. . . . Change is not treason. I suppose that's what I would like to say. Change is a process of growth. . . ."

But Slater also recognized the anachronistic qualities of the new Eldridge in his lead sentences: "Like the ghost of Christmas past, Eldridge Cleaver is among us again, stalking the edges of memory. In the old days, exuding an almost biblical rage, he spoke to thousands. . . ." And he noted Nat Hentoff's characterization of Eldridge as ". . . this veritable bicentennial bell-ringer of the virtues . . . of America." Slater wrote that the new Eldridge "is a stranger to most of those who idolized him in the late sixties. Is he now, in some way, a stranger unto himself?"

The answer, of course, was yes.

Other newsmen weren't so perceptive or they deliberately shied away from getting too subjective with Eldridge. They felt that the best way to assess this returned exile was to keep him at an objective distance and see how he squirmed on the media's proverbial "hook." Throughout the summer of 1976, Eldridge's legal dealings led him first to discard his attorney George Higgins. He lived in Boston and had insurmountable difficulties in dealing with Eldridge who was three thousand miles away in Oakland. Then there was a delay of weeks while he searched for a new lawyer and ways to pay the high legal fees. He had to watch the valiant efforts of Kathleen to try, without great success, to boost the coffers of the Cleaver Legal Defense Fund. Finally he got a new lawyer. Through all the legal musical chairs, Eldridge did manage to gain his release on $100,000 bail in mid-August. One of his first appearances afterward was on NBC's "Meet The Press," August 29.

Moderated by Bill Monroe, the three panelists that day—Ford Rowan of NBC News, Paul Delaney of *The New York Times* and Robert Novack of *Chicago Sun-Times*—tried to hoist Eldridge on his own old Panther petard. In some two dozen questions showing in my printed copy of that program, the three pinned him down hard on his politics, old and new. Eldridge, who has said many times he enjoyed talking politics, took all their questions and fielded them well.

Q. Some of your former colleagues said you made some kind of deal with the government to stay out of jail—is that true? **A.** The fact that I didn't stay out of jail should explain very quickly, that it wasn't true. I had some very deep transformations in my own personal life and my outlook on life which they didn't understand. (No one on the panel followed up on what the transformations were.)

Q. In *Soul on Ice*, you said that if you had followed the advice of the authorities you could have stayed out of prison, but that you would have been less of a man and would be weakened. Now that you've come back and face the possibility of going to prison, do you feel weaker and less of a man? **A.** I have never felt stronger and more manly in my life. The prison system is there to change your behavior, to rehabilitate people, but I don't feel that I am in need of any rehabilitation, and that I have no need to be in prison.

Q. You said no deal had been made. Nevertheless, a lot of blacks believe a deal has been made. They are puzzled by your return and your new posture. How do you explain it? **A.** I think a lot of people are not used to seeing someone voluntarily surrender, knowing that they will go immediately into jail. In most cases you see people, as I did, running away. . . . I had a change . . . toward how change should be approached in this country . . . [which] came particularly because the country began to react to some of the problems . . . posed . . . like the war . . . terminating . . . the Senate and the courts . . . beginning to deal with . . . Watergate . . . and progress being made by black people . . . in the political life of this country. . . . This indicates that other people should be more open and considerate, willing, really, to bend a little bit in order to facilitate things.

Q. In an interview with *Rolling Stone* magazine, you praised the military, but also proposed a major purge of the officers, a rewriting of the manuals, and called for moving on the military because without their support there would be no revolution. What do you have in mind for the military in some kind of revolution? **A.** I don't have any program in mind for the use of the

American military to conduct revolution. . . . I was talking about . . . the military . . . [being] constitutionally bound to carry out the orders and direction of the civilian government. A lot of people during the war tended to blame the Pentagon or the military for the war itself, when in fact they were carrying out the orders of civilian government. Some excesses were coming out of the Pentagon. . . . I base my call for removal of the officers responsible for that. . . . My observations around the world are that people inside of the military establishments . . . are also humans. And to just take a position that the military people are not interested in progress and change . . . is a big mistake.

Q. Is your only criticism of Chinese government that former President Nixon shook hands with the Chinese? **A.** This is not the basis of my total criticism . . . My major criticism with all communist governments has to do with their lack of any machinery through which people are able to bring [their] will to bear on the decision-making process. . . . They have dictatorial . . . regimes which, by their very nature, are oppressive. . . .

Q. You said you think you will win your court case on the 1968 shoot-out charges. What makes you think so? **A.** As I told you, as my attorney told you before this program, the judge . . . presiding . . . has imposed a very stringent gag rule, and I am not allowed to discuss this. But . . . my co-defendants went to trial at a time when people were not willing to question the behavior and . . . motivation of police . . . before the

241

exposes of . . . Watergate . . . and the COINTELPRO activities . . . I am coming to trial in a very different climate. I feel I will be able to have a fair day in court and I think I will be vindicated. . . ."

Q. You used to be a very violent man. In view of this background, wouldn't some people believe that . . . your present posture . . . might be a big con game to set up public opinion to help you in your trial? **A.** I am sure that there are a lot of cynical people who immediately seek to find an interpretation of that sort. . . . I could have continued to live in France, but I wanted to come back and straighten out my life, to clear myself . . . to raise my family in the United States. Those who are looking for some hidden motivation or some secret deal or reason, they are welcome to look. I am willing to stand examination.

Q. During your time overseas the American National Security Agency had your name on a watch list and spied on your movements. [We] are trying to probe your feelings about a government that you have come back to and embraced when . . . you have reason . . . to dislike some of its tactics. **A.** I do dislike the illegal activities carried out . . . but other countries do the same thing. . . . I think [our prison system, police agencies, FBI and CIA] stack up very favorably when you compare them with some of the others. . . .

Q. Mr. Gloster Current of the NAACP has called you a "creature of the media," and has said that you have "contributed absolutely nothing" to the black movement. Do you feel that you personally or the Black Panther Party can take any credit for improvement in the lot of black people? **A.** It's a kind of complicated question. . . . I've read that [Mr. Current's statement] before—it is for other people to judge whether or not the Black Panther Party contributed anything to the progress of black people in this country, or whether I contributed. Personally, I feel that we played a particular role at a particular time in history, and I am quite satisfied . . . there was some good in what we did and there was some bad.

Q. What was the bad? **A.** I think that we were a little naive in our approach . . . that we were excessive in our language . . . that we scared a lot of people, not so much by our practice, our activities, but by the way that we described certain situations, and if I had it to do all over again, with hindsight, I would do it differently.

Q. If you lose your case and are sentenced to a long jail term, what might be your future? And what might it be if you win your case and go free? **A.** One thing that happened to me during the period I was abroad and really was the underlying reason I was able to find the courage and strength to return and go to prison is that I experienced religious conversion. I have become a Christian, and anything that I do in the future has to take that into consideration. I am a person with a heart full of goodwill. I am interested in whatever good contribution that I can make. If it is the will of the Lord that I go to prison, that I lose my case, then I will go to prison and whatever happens there will happen there. If I am acquitted, as I feel that I will be, as I feel would be just, then I will do whatever work the Lord brings to me, so it is as simple as that.

Q. Is that likely to be writing or lecturing?
A. I think that as long as I am able I will write and I will lecture, yes.

Q. What about politics?   **A.** I like to criticize politicians, you know. I like to observe the political process. . . . I have no political aspirations of my own.

Q. It is very hard to understand people who have undergone conversions. You said if you had to do it over again you would do it differently. Once you said, "A dead pig is the best pig of all," referring to policemen. "We encourage people to kill them." Is that the kind of thing you would not do if you had to do it again? How much of *Soul on Ice* would you just throw away?   **A.** I wouldn't throw *Soul on Ice* away at all. I would leave it on the shelf for people to read because I think it belongs in a certain time frame and period of history. But I certainly don't really remember making that statement, but it is a vintage Panther of the sixties, so I think this would be something I would avoid—except the reprehensible behavior of the police and . . . during that period cannot be condoned. . . .

So the "private" Eldridge had finally caught up with the "public" Eldridge. He was able to bring the experience of the night on the balcony in southern France out into the open. Yet, these secular newsmen on one of the nation's top televised news programs admitted, "It is hard to understand people who have undergone conversions." They didn't know how to cope with Christians, let alone this once awesome Panther leader who was now saying he was one. They had enough to deal with trying to cope with the mind-boggling switch in his political beliefs. Of course, on their own level, the questions the "Meet The Press" panelists did ask were vital in assessing and understanding the new Eldridge.

However, if Jesus Christ was a mystery to the panelists and other newsmen, and the curious, skeptical world at large, he wasn't to Eldridge. In the months between November, 1975, and his appearance on "Meet The Press" in August, 1976, Eldridge had been dealing earnestly with the intimate matters of his private world. The revolutionary had come home to Babylon; the inner man returned from an even longer, more distant exile, to a whole new world. This man was the *really new* Eldridge Cleaver.

The journey of *this* new man is a story all its own.

BOOK FIVE

THE NEW MAN

CHAPTER ONE

SAN DIEGO

By his second night home in Babylon, Eldridge was in the Federal Corrections Institute in San Diego. He had come full circle. He had traveled around the world, gone down a thousand blind alleys, exhausted all the false gods he could find, and here he was, a quarter of a century later, only a few miles from where his childhood vandalism in Los Angeles had started him on the round of juvenile halls and prison cells.

Only a few weeks had passed since his balcony experience and Eldridge was already in the dark spot on that shaft of light. And he was dealing with it—with the solution: surrender. He was dealing with *surrender*, an act he had run all his life to keep from doing. The outward aspects of this had already been dealt with. He had turned himself over to the authorities and was in custody, trial-bound at last. The world beyond his jail cell was judging him on those grounds, on what people could see. The inner surrender though, the hidden part known only to Eldridge, was going through its own processing; Eldridge was dealing with that almost separately, although he knew both parts of this final surrender were related. He'd made the decision in both areas, but with the inner one he still had some wrestling to do.

He had been totally committed to whatever course of action he had chosen. He had read and studied and thought until he had mastered whatever it was, like Marx for example, and then he had moved. But this inner matter was radically different from anything before. In this, it seemed as though he had committed himself first and now was trying to understand.

There was no way he could *not* have done what he had done, not after the trauma of that Mediterranean night. He realized that, but he didn't understand it. He was turned around in his shoes, all right; but, oddly, they were strangely comfortable. He wanted to know why. Here he was, back in jail, but without any rage. He felt peaceful. He still yearned for freedom, true; but somehow, he was content, knowing he was doing the right thing. He searched himself to know why.

He knew one thing for sure: the traumatic experience on the balcony had left his mind pounds lighter, as though a heavy burden had been lifted from him. He had an abiding sense of serenity which he had never known before. And now that he was in the dark spot on that shaft of light, he was sure he was following the right course at last, wherever it might lead. But even with that assurance, he kept asking, Why?

And another thing was sure: Nobody on earth ever again would accuse him or convict him as he had been accused and convicted that night. The charges God had brought against him that night would *never* be exceeded—or even matched—by any district attorney

250

or grand jury. God had leveled the accusations at him with matchless accuracy and wisdom, by bringing Eldridge to where he himself admitted to them. Conscience? Yes, of course. Man's conscience is God's courtroom.

Eldridge must have missed Kathleen and Maceo and Joju while he was in San Diego. They were in his mind constantly; they were why he was here. His love for them had been a vital part of the cause of his own misery, of his coming to his own dead end, and of his subsequent decision to surrender.

Also strange was his lack of wrath and rage. Instead of boiling fury he had this sense of peace and a growing awareness of love—at least an awareness of his lack of hate—for everyone. Then, too, the enjoyment of having friends, of caring for someone whom you knew cared for you, was an experience he had confessed to Gene Marine. That was something he'd found during the Panther years. Having been without friends in the French exile and now once again behind bars, plus being turned around in his shoes, and trying to *understand* his experience on the balcony—now, he yearned for friendship more than ever. The confinement, which he welcomed in a strange way because it gave him time and solitude in which to think, made him also welcome anyone who came to see him.

So when one day a former black militant turned preacher whom Eldridge knew asked for permission to come in to see him, Eldridge agreed. The man entered carrying a Bible and they talked, the man asked, "What's happened with you, man? I know something's up," with all the news he'd heard about Eldridge's return.

Suddenly, out of context, he said, "Eldridge Cleaver, I want to do something. I don't want you to get mad at me. Just listen. You don't have to respond."

Eldridge listened. Then the man said: "Eldridge Cleaver, this is Jesus Christ. Jesus Christ, this is Eldridge Cleaver."

That penetrated Eldridge. He got angry with the man. How could this man get that presumptuous and talk like that to him? Eldridge knew about the Bible. He knew Christ was spoken of there. Who was this man to presume to introduce him to Jesus Christ? Eldridge felt like grabbing him, but he subdued the impulse. He did tell the man it was pretty arrogant for him to speak like that, but they talked some more before the man finally left. He never returned.

Afterwards, Eldridge mused over the words, alternately furious and troubled by the experience. Later, he got to thinking that he guessed the man knew what he was doing, but the *way* he handled that "introduction" was way out in left field some place.

Others, not so nettling, also visited. The Correctional Center's Protestant chaplain, Rev. David DeHaas, stopped by to chat and the Rev. George Stevens, a local member of a group called the "God Squad" dropped in.

* * * *

All this was part of Eldridge's entry into a totally new world: Life with Jesus Christ, peopled by folks who carried Bibles and quoted Scriptures and talked about God in a way he hadn't heard since childhood when he used to listen to his mother or his Sunday school teachers. Funny how familiar some of the Bible verses were, the way the Lord's Prayer and the 23rd Psalm had been on the balcony that night. They were like reminders, as though he suddenly found himself walking on a long-forgotten but familiar path. Now, though, what these people were saying was new, different, more meaningful. He listened carefully. What he heard took some of the sourness from the incident where the man "introduced" him to Jesus Christ.

* * * *

In a way, it was a tailor-made situation. There seems something appropriate in Eldridge's complete change of outlook occurring in prison. What had been started on the balcony was completed in jail—as much as anything can ever be completed, considering life is a constant process of change, of becoming. It had been in prison that Eldridge had become first a determined Communist, then atheist, then iconoclast, Black Muslim, radical, committed revolutionary. He would commit himself to Christ on that same "home territory." A crazy, mixed-up, turned-around-in-your-shoes thought: to find freedom in jail. Eldridge's lawyers outside were using every point of law to free him from prison. God was using prison to free Eldridge from his old self.

In the process, Eldridge would find that the world is full of Christians—well, if not full, certainly it contains more than he'd ever been aware of before. They were everywhere, coming into jail to visit, or already there serving time. His stay at the San Diego facility was only the beginning. What he would find in Oakland, when they moved him up there early in January, 1976, would boggle his mind. He had always understood that Oakland would be the ultimate destination of his homecoming, because that was where he would ultimately have his day in court. He just never imagined he would be returning there in this fashion.

CHAPTER TWO

OAKLAND

The Alameda County Courthouse Jail sits on the top floors of the Superior Court maze, District Attorney's offices and labyrinth of county records and election bureaus. When you get out of the elevator on the tenth floor you're in a cramped entryway with a visitor's sign-in desk to your right, the administrative offices directly ahead behind heavy bulletproof windows, and the prisoners' tanks to your right and left down narrow, poorly lighted corridors. You talk to whatever prisoner you've come to see over telephones with cords so short you have to bend over to talk and listen; and you can see each other through a thick pane of glass not much larger than a good-sized rear-view mirror. You can see into the tank, the large recreation room bordered by several cells. Beyond and upstairs, out of sight, are other tanks with other prisoners, the jail infirmary, "The Hole," the usual prison accouterments.

Sometime during January 7, 1976, a car bearing Eldridge drove down the ramp to the security entrance of the jail in the basement of the courthouse.

Handcuffed, with a chain from the cuffs to another around his waist, he was led up the elevator to the "penthouse" jails above. After being processed, he was placed in "A" tank with half a dozen or so other inmates.

Since the news of his return to the U.S. a few weeks before I had developed a growing interest in Eldridge. Doing a story for the *Tri-Valley Herald* of which I was associate editor was out of the question since Oakland was out of our circulation area. But as a free-lance correspondent on the side for the *National Courier*, I had what sounded like a good story. The notorious Eldridge Cleaver was back in the country, and now, close by. What kept fibrillating news-wise was that behind his return from exile, knowing he was going to prison, *had* to be some sort of drastic change.

My curiosity didn't motivate me at first, but within a few weeks, with the continuing local interest, it did. Also, Bill Worrell, then assistant national editor of the *Courier*, called about a rumor that Eldridge had accepted Christ. Had I heard anything about it? No. Would I check? Yes.

I renewed acquaintances with a number of people I'd known from two years of covering county police beats through the Sheriff Department's Rehabilitation Center at Santa Rita about thirty miles southeast of Oakland. In the process I ran across an old political friend, Cliff Harbaugh, who, in the years since we'd last talked, had become a Christian and was now a prison evangelist. He turned out to be a wealth of information about what was going on down at the courthouse jail. He visited there regularly at least once a week.

Yes, he knew about Eldridge. Yes, Eldridge was undergoing a profound religious experience. No,

Harbaugh didn't think Eldridge had turned his life over to Jesus Christ, despite the stories. What stories? Oh, haven't you heard? Eldridge is really upset that any word about his being converted has been leaked to the press.

The upsetting stories appeared first in Southern California in mid-March, but they reported events that occurred, they stated, in late January and February.

The first, in the *San Diego Evening Tribune* on March 13, 1976, was headlined: " 'God Squad' Gets to Cleaver." The story led off with, "The God Squad got to Eldridge Cleaver two months ago and he became a Christian." The story's main source was the Rev. Glenn Morrison, head of Follow Up Ministries, known affectionately among jail inmates as the "God Squad."

"Mr. Morrison," according to the *Tribune*, "said Cleaver embraced Christianity shortly after entering the Alameda County Courthouse Jail in early January where Mr. Morrison is chaplain. . . . 'I just helped him put the pieces together,' Mr. Morrison said. . . . 'He knew he had a spiritual vacuum in his life and came to realize that Jesus Christ could fill it. I feel the man is a genuine Christian. He is not ready to talk about it now because he doesn't want to be labeled as a hypocritical Christian. . . .'"

The *Tribune* also mentioned the men who had talked to Eldridge in San Diego.

The second story, on March 15, 1976, by Russell Chandler of the *Los Angeles Times*, came under the headline; "Conversions To Christ—A Prison Revival." It dealt with "conversions" among "even the most notorious" convicts such as three members of the Charles Manson family involved in the shocking

Tate-La Bianca slayings in Southern California, even noting that the mystic, monk-like leader Charles Manson himself "appeared open to the Christian faith," according to San Quentin prison chaplain Harry Howard. Other Manson clan members, Susan Atkins and Charles (Tex) Watson, were also telling reporters that they had been born again, with Miss Atkins even being baptized in the California Institution for Woman at Frontera, and Watson being a "deacon" in the inmate church at the California Men's Colony at San Luis Obispo and song leader for Chaplain Ray Hoekstra's daily prison broadcasts carried on 102 radio stations.

Chandler's story noted how skeptics consider that "such jailhouse conversions" are really "calculated to win favor with parole boards, chaplains and wardens, and even to cover up drug-passing." But former hatchet man for President Nixon, Charles Colson, was quoted as saying, "Miracles are happening. Lives are being changed on a lasting basis." Colson had just received approval from the Federal Bureau of Prisons to institute a training program for convict evangelists to allow inmates to be released from prison in order to study so that they could become more effective in the prison spiritual work.

The *Times* touched on Eldridge, too. News of his "conversion" reached the outside world "through a friend who visited the former Panther in his Oakland jail cell at Cleaver's request.

"The visitor, a former Panther himself who is now a deacon in Calvary Baptist Church, San Diego, related to his pastor the story of Cleaver's conversion. The minister, the Rev. Shadrach Meshach Lockeridge, recounted it on February 4 at a gathering of 600 Baptist ministers in Jackson, Mississippi.

"Sources close to Cleaver say he does not want to say anything public about his spiritual experiences now because he does not want to use it as a lever to secure favors or to appear that he is doing so.

"But a chaplain who works with inmates in the Alameda County jails said he met Cleaver in the Oakland jail in January, where he had been placed in a tank with a strong Christian convict. . . ."

Both the *Tribune* and the *Times* referred to this "strong Christian convict" as a "long-time bitter enemy" of Cleaver's since the two men had served time in San Quentin together.

The stories contained truths and errors. It was true Eldridge didn't want his "conversion" made public because he didn't want to be labeled hypocritical or that he was trying to secure favors regarding his upcoming trial. But that this "conversion" business had occurred in late January or February was inaccurate, because it was premature. Also, the "strong Christian convict" was not a bitter enemy of Eldridge's.

He was Frank Gordon, a bearded middle-aged prison-wise con who had spent thirty-three of his forty-nine years behind bars. A four-time loser who had violated parole by bad-check writing, Gordon was back in jail in 1975. He was kicking out anybody who tried to talk to him about the Christian faith; he bragged that he had read the Bible through seven times, twice while he was on death row, and he knew what it said. But it had never done anything for him, so he didn't want to hear any more about it.

Into Gordon's tank one day early in 1975 came Bill Kocourek, a silver-haired ex-Navy chief with some twenty years of military service who had just been arrested for murdering his wife. Terribly remorseful, readily admitting his guilt, torn apart inside and his life a shambles, Billy shook his head at an evangelist's offer of help. He told the evangelist, Cliff Harbaugh, that nothing could pray him out of purgatory for what he had done. It was too late for any kind of help. Yet, according to Harbaugh later, it was only a few days afterwards that Kocourek changed drastically, feeling that perhaps God might hold some answer for him after all, and followed the biblical instructions to turn his life—what was left of it—over to Jesus Christ.

In the course of their daily associations Kocourek and Gordon got to talking about religion and Kocourek explained to Gordon what had just happened to him. A "believer," Kocourek was experiencing a peace of mind that somehow got to the rabidly antagonistic Gordon and convinced him that what Kocourek had was real. The two became fast friends and joined the other Christians in the tank at the weekly church services and Bible classes held by various visiting evangelists, most notably Rev. Morrison's "God Squad."

Just prior to Eldridge's arrival in January, 1976, Kocourek and Gordon had been separated because prison officials felt they were "getting too close." When a prison protest almost broke out, the two were considered the key plotters. Gordon was thrown into the "hole" as punishment and had just come out, transferred into "A" tank, when Eldridge appeared.

Though still a new Christian, Gordon began talking religion and faith to Eldridge. It started apparently when Eldridge walked by Gordon's cell one day and saw him reading his Bible and called in, "So you found it there, huh?" Gordon nodded and from then on Eldridge plied him with questions.

Eldridge, according to Gordon's recollection, admitted Jesus Christ was a great teacher, a remarkably wise man, and a great revolutionary. But Eldridge couldn't buy the bit about "Christ dying for my sins," and about His resurrection. In the very short time before Gordon was transferred to Vacaville he and Eldridge went through the Bible and talked about what faith really meant.

After Gordon's departure, Eldridge was transferred to "B" tank where he came in contact with Kocourek and the Christian convicts there. Among these was a young man named Rick Karr, who was currently being tried for his part in a murder. About the time of Eldridge's arrival Karr had been found guilty and sentenced to the gas chamber; he was still awaiting his final departure to death row at San Quentin.

Kocourek and Karr were among those on whom Eldridge laid his persistent biblical questions. Like Gordon before them and like the regularly visiting evangelists, these two went through the Bible explaining Scriptures here and there to try to dispel Eldridge's nagging doubts.

Gordon and Eldridge confirm one another's recollections about those first days in "A" tank. Gordon says Eldridge kept a safe distance for the first week or so from the "God Squad" evangelists and prisoners who gathered for the Sunday services. Eldridge admits being leery about getting too close, too involved with any of it.

To church audiences Eldridge says: "I'd stand back and look at them. I didn't want to go up to the table where they would be talking, because what they used to do was join hands and close their eyes and say a little prayer, pray together.

"I couldn't get hung up in that because, first of all, I'd be embarrassed to be praying like that, and secondly, I wasn't particularly fond of closing my eyes with all those other guys standing around there in the tank. Everybody ends up praying—bowing their heads and kind of looking with one eye over their shoulder."

It was not until after Eldridge moved into "B" tank that he began to warm up. His talks with Gordon, Kocourek and Karr, and sometimes with other prisoners, were having some effect. His curiosity was piqued more and more. He found himself going through the Bible on his own, trying to get all the pieces to fit. He'd long since discarded Marx and Engels and Fanon, and Bakunin and Nechayev's *Catechism of the Revolutionist*—his favorite prison-reading in earlier prison years. The Bible held his curiosity now, and he was determined to master it as he had mastered all the revolutionary theories.

One day, Eldridge says, the time came when he sat down with the others during one of the religious services. ". . . Something was bothering me, and I just couldn't stay away. So finally one day I went and sat down. . . ." Maybe he'd hear something that would help fill the growing emptiness inside, a void deeper even than the disillusionment he'd felt in France during all the months before the balcony episode. That night had told him what he had to do, that he had to surrender and cast aside all the former theories and causes he'd held on to; that he had to give himself up and come home from exile. But he was empty inside. Nothing held him up anymore. Just a vast empty space, as though something had vacuumed his mind. He needed something to fill it up.

After one of the meetings, "I got the minister [Rev. Glenn Morrison] and I told him what had been going on in my life. I'd kind of boiled it down to where I knew I needed a relationship with God.

"There was in me this vacuum, this gulf, that had to be filled. He began to talk to me in a very clear way about how that can only be filled by God, by God through His Son Jesus Christ."

It was the same story Eldridge had been hearing from all the others when he asked questions.

". . . And so everything began, slowly, to fall into place. Things that had been happening to me began to make more sense. . . ."

Eldridge's presence in Oakland was public knowledge and visitors would come in from time to time asking permission to see him. He nearly always gave it. Sometimes, though, these talks, often with complete strangers, led to some strange experiences, some of which cast new doubts into his already questioning mind about Christianity. People who said they believed in the Bible and knew all about Jesus Christ, got pretty kooky. One day a lady came in and talked to him over one of the short-cord prison phones. Eldridge could see her through the small visitor's window. She raised her hand as she said, "We're going to pray together. If you really believe, these walls are going to fall down."

They prayed, and the walls didn't fall down, so she muttered through the phone, "You don't believe," and hung up and split. That gave Eldridge added skepticism about all that he'd been hearing from the preachers and others.

* * * *

Other things were impinging sharply on Eldridge all
this time, also. His upcoming trial, scheduled then for
sometime in June, was jammed with complications. His
case rested, among other things, on proving that the
Panthers had not ambushed the Oakland police back in
that April, 1968 shoot-out as police claimed. The core
charges against him involved alleging that he had
assaulted police officers with a deadly weapon and had
attempted to kill officers engaged in the gun battle. His
defense, based on self-defense, involved proving that
the police, not the Panthers in ambush, had provoked
the fight, as part of a design of deliberate harassment
against radical groups crying revolution. And this, in
turn, involved filing discovery motions to secure
federal records containing information already
released, plus others still withheld, of the Senate
investigations of the FBI's Counter Intelligence
Program (COINTELPRO) which disclosed that,
indeed, a nationwide operation against subversive,
revolutionary groups had existed in the late sixties.
The case went through a series of delays as
Eldridge's attorneys maneuvered with the prosecution
locally and with federal authorities in Washington.
Eldridge had developed a strong sense of how his
defense should be conducted, and not all of the ploys by
his attorneys sat right with him. Money was always a
problem also. He was already tens of thousands of
dollars in debt from massive legal fees.
Debts presented an ever-present specter. Kathleen

was busy traveling all over the country on speaking engagements, explaining Eldridge's turnabout politics, trying to get financial support for his defense fund. One estimate given me speculated that legal fees would eventually go as high as $250,000. By mid-April, 1976, the *San Francisco Examiner* reported that no more than $5,000 had been raised. Personal finances were in desperate shape, too. It cost money for Kathleen's extensive travel on Eldridge's behalf.

In addition there were other, strategic considerations. The Cleavers kept exploring old friends, old acquaintances, old supporters who might still be loyal enough to help Eldridge. Some of these dropped by the wayside. Many old supporters, some of whom had washed their hands of Eldridge while he was still in France seeking aid in returning to the United States, wanted nothing to do with him.

Plus there was the continuing open criticism from many segments of the public. The Black Panthers who back in January had called him "the black man's Patty Hearst," were saying by April that Eldridge was finking to the Senate Judiciary Internal Security Subcommittee charging that he had been active and willing agent in the FBI's COINTELPRO operations, "to destroy black organizations by creating internal dissensions."

There were also some rumors of death threats against Eldridge, coming from within the prison system itself, from some convicts incensed by his turnabout who figured he deserved vengeful justice. Through fellow inmates he trusted and others who could see his sincerity, he passed word along the line that he wasn't seeking any deals, that what was happening to him was in earnest—a deep inexorable change about which he was as honest as he had ever been about his former revolutionary views.

* * * *

Sometime during all these developing events in the spring of 1976, Eldridge's thinking finally jumped the mental obstacles he harbored about Christ. He moved from looking at Jesus as a historical figure, teacher, revolutionary, and ordinary man to the more mystical, spiritual aspects of the Christian faith, the reality obtained in the Gospels, and finally, to the meaning of the cross. At last he accepted Jesus' redemptive work at Calvary, believing that Christ had, indeed, been resurrected. What Eldridge found in the Gospels became more real to him than anything in his life, and Eldridge had always been one who dealt in reality as he felt he saw it.

All that everyone had been saying in response to his questioning came down on him one night when he was alone in his cell.

"Finally," he describes, "one night I was lying in my bed—this was after talking to these ministers and them telling me what I had to do, what should be done, urging me along and bringing me along—for the first time, I really prayed, and for myself, and for Jesus to really take control of my life and to come into my heart and become my personal Savior." What's this? Eldridge Cleaver, the inflammatory revolutionist, talking gibberish, old-time, street-corner, camp-ground, tent-meeting religion? Incredible!

Later he said, "There are so many things that just

amaze me. I haven't met one single person, since that night on the balcony, that I don't love. I mean, I'm looking for someone that I'm liable to have that old feeling towards. But I haven't found one single person that I don't love."

That was how it was to come out later. However, in May, 1976, he was telling the *National Courier* that he wasn't in a "hallelujah, fundamentalist kind of bag." But shortly after that he told me in one of our conversations through the jail peep-hole that, "You know, there are a lot of things, that I can see now, I should have included in that article. A lot of things I should have said. So many amazing things have been happening to me—phew! I can't keep up with them all."

Still, however, Eldridge seemed reluctant to open up. He was undergoing a lot of self-consciousness and *was* reluctant to blurt out everything. Inside he knew he had given control of his life over to Someone else. But telling this to other people—the way you pass the time of day—he felt would create disbelief, ridicule, joshing and criticism. He had to carry his new confession and beliefs around silently for a while yet. He had to wear his new inner man until he felt comfortable before he could disclose himself to others.

Amazing things were beginning to happen, all right. By early summer Eldridge settled on Patrick Hallinan as his new attorney. Moves were being made to deal with the parole board so that he could be released on bail, even if it was as much as $100,000. They managed to get San Francisco Supervisor Quentin Kopp, a respected lawyer in his own right, to plead his parole case for him.

Kopp argued for a writ of habeas corpus on the

grounds Eldridge had already served more time than
called for in the state statutes applying to his original
sentence prior to 1968. A new state law had recently
done away with the old indeterminate sentence
provision which allowed the California Adult Authority
to have such absolute power over convicts' sentences
and parolees' lives. The parole board had been
reviewing the status of the state's some forty thousand
prisoners, and conducting hearings to see whether
prison terms should be abbreviated and whether some
should be allowed freedom. No longer could a man be
thrust into prison for an unnamed length of time within
the limits of the state statutes. A convicted man had to
be told of his "primary term," the sentence being
determined solely on pre-conviction factors and
relating to the defendant at the time of his conviction.
Moreover, this primary term could no longer be
increased because of subsequent behavior deemed
"punishable" by the parole board.

On these grounds, Alameda County Superior Court
Judge Spurgeon Avakian ruled in July that it appeared
Eldridge had served more time than his original
sentence warranted, and ordered the Adult Authority
to grant him a hearing within the next thirty days to
determine if he could be released on bail. The board
obeyed, and on Friday, August 13, 1976, with bail
posted by friends, notably Art DeMoss, a Philadelphia
insurance executive, Eldridge walked out of jail a free
man.

Evangelist Cliff Harbaugh visited Eldridge the day
the bail was being posted, bringing with him the latest
in a series of Bible studies he and Eldridge had been
discussing. Harbaugh came in cold, knowing nothing of

Eldridge's having been down for a bail hearing earlier that day. Harbaugh had known negotiations were going on for the $100,000 bail, that part of the bonds supplied as surety had not been accepted, and that a bail bondsman had been contacted to supply amounts needed beyond Art Demoss's contribution of the major portion, but he was unaware of exactly where matters stood. However, he detected Eldridge was somewhat nervous and preoccupied, not as interested as usual in the Bible studies.

Finally Eldridge told Harbaugh he was waiting to hear about the bail. He also expressed some other concerns.

"What'll I tell the reporters? What should I say when they ask me about being a Christian?" he asked.

"Tell 'em whatever you want, that you've been born again, or whatever you want to use. Tell 'em the truth. That's all you have to do."

That was the first time Harbaugh had heard the nitty-gritty about Eldridge's new life personally, from his own lips. Always there had been some questions; rumors, yes; affirmations, yes; but always, Harbaugh had felt some doubts as to whether Eldridge was really on the Christian side of the fence.

But here it was. Here, dressed in prison whites, sitting beside him in "B" tank, Harbaugh was looking at a new man. Eldridge Cleaver had been reborn.

CHAPTER THREE

FREE AT LAST?

If they had wondered where Eldridge was coming from when he returned from exile in November, 1975, newsmen shook their heads in sheer bewilderment beginning August 13, 1976.

At 6:58 P.M. that day, according to the *San Francisco Chronicle*, "Eldridge Cleaver emerged from Elevator No. 3 on the first floor of the Alameda County Courthouse, free for the first time since last November."

Eldridge had exchanged his white jail togs for a white suit, brown tie and light shirt. He walked over to the "hastily produced table containing eleven microphones and said firmly:

"I have no apprehension about being on the street."

Replying to questions about the Black Panthers' accusations that he had become a "counter-revolutionary," Eldridge explained, "People have misunderstood my position. When I left the country in 1968 . . . it was because the FBI and the CIA had joined in a conspiracy to destroy the Black Panther Party."

Was he back on the old kick? Or were reporters still unwilling to let the "old man" Cleaver die, to rest in peace?

How did he feel now that he was free on bail? he was asked.

"I just want to thank God for the changes in my life," he replied. "And I want to thank my Christian brothers and sisters for all their prayers. Without them I wouldn't be out of jail today."

For some reason, the *Chronicle* didn't print that last comment. Maybe their reporter didn't hear it. Maybe Eldridge said it to one or two in the huddle of thronging reporters. But he said it, and it was a preamble to all his public statements which have boggled minds since.

The *Chronicle* did run a photo of Eldridge which underscores his words—and his happiness. The usually inscrutable face with its deadpan expression is split into a smile and Eldridge has his hands together, cupped in a gesture that would always tickle later audiences: an infectious little round of self-applause, as though he clapped in glee at this new inner man of his.

In one sense, Eldridge literally exploded from jail into the free, open air once more. Kathleen, in a dark jacket over a light-colored pants suit with a colorful scarf around her neck was radiant as she and Eldridge, with a thick expandable file tucked under each arm made their way through the reporters and cameramen to a car taking them home. They have seldom stopped moving since that bail-getaway day.

Before Labor Day he appeared on "Meet The Press," and "Good Morning, America." At about the same time Henry Mitchell in the *Washington Post* quoted

Eldridge in response to the perennial question about whether or not he had made a deal to gain his freedom: ". . . The only deal I made, coming back to face arrest, was for the federal government to guarantee my personal safety against the Oakland police and the Alameda County sheriff's office. That's the only deal there was.

"Unless you count another thing . . . I made a deal with Jesus Christ."

There it was again, the astounding old-time religion vocabulary.

By September 5, the *Philadelphia Inquirer* published Mitchell's story, adding some final parenthetical paragraphs about Art DeMoss's role in providing Eldridge's bail.

"DeMoss said he decided to provide the $41,000 bail [his portion of the $100,000 total] because Cleaver's discovery of Christ paralleled his own discovery twenty-five years ago. 'I wrote welcoming him into the Lord's family and have visited him in prison,' said DeMoss. 'I am convinced that the change in Eldridge is real and genuine.' "

The cover of the September issue of *San Diego Church News* ran a large photo of Eldridge and led off its main story with his quote: " 'It's too bad it took me 20 years to get to this point.' " He had told that to Ken Overstreet, executive director of Youth for Christ in San Diego, in an interview just before his release.

The story's headline, "Eldridge Cleaver Freed By Christians," adds an as-yet-unmentioned aspect of the Oakland jail period. The $100,000 bail was paid for "by contributions from the Christian community.

"Christians from all over the country started

corresponding with Eldridge when the word came out that he had become a Christian. Maxine Snyder, his attorney in prison, told Ken that Cleaver spent most of his time answering his many letters from Christians instead of taking care of all the legal documents she needed to facilitate his release."

The *Church News* also quoted San Diego's God Squad Chaplain George Stevans who had visited him at the Metropolitan Correctional Institute there: "I knew then that Eldridge was at the doorway of accepting Christ." When Stevans visited Eldridge in Oakland in February, he "knew that Eldridge had accepted Christ."

Who knows exactly when a man accepts Christ? Others who know Eldridge feel that this occurred later. What the discrepancy in the dates seems most to prove, however, is that the press was not around to report on it. The best investigative newsman in the world can't invade the holy privacy between a man and his God. It's a one-to-one relationship, "hidden with Christ in God," sub-surface, down in the labyrinthian passageways of the soul and spirit. It was down there that the spring thaw had finally come to Eldridge's former ice-bound self.

The melting has flooded into everything that Eldridge has done or said since, as the public has become so increasingly aware. The media has done its best to get at *this*, although sometimes there seems a reluctance. I have a photocopy of a *New York Times* galley-print-out, headlined; "Cleaver 'Testifies' As An Evangelical." Above the headline is an editorial stamp: "Killed by Editor." I don't know if the story ran on October 13, 1976, as indicated it was scheduled for, or later—or never.

But the *Washington Star* ran a story on its October 9 church page which, although it has an embarrassing flaw, tells it like Eldridge says it these days: "Eldredge (sic) Cleaver: 'I saw Jesus in the Moon.' "

The moon night. Eldridge refers to that as his conversion experience. Well, he should know. That was another time the press wasn't present.

Back in September, Russ Chandler, religious writer for the Los Angeles *Times*, attended a two-hour press conference held by Eldridge, and wrote in the *Times* on September 14, 1976, that Eldridge was "going on the lecture circuit." Chandler wrote that Eldridge had already been busily meeting with Billy Graham in San Diego, Charles Colson in Washington, and had signed with a national speakers' bureau and with a major publishing house for a book "detailing his 'philosophical and spiritual evolution.' "

His pace is incredible. By January, 1977, he had spoken at some twenty colleges and universities, including Indiana, Northwestern, and Tulane; had appeared on TV with Susan Brownmiller; was busy talking to Rotary clubs, of all things, in the San Francisco Bay Area, and to churches all over the country. He had been given the full pulpit time in November on Dr. Robert Schuller's "Hour of Power" televised Sunday church service; had appeared on the "700 Club," and the "PTL Club" TV programs; had jammed an audience of nearly fifteen-hundred into the sanctuary of the Walnut Creek Presbyterian Church in California which was built to hold only about nine-hundred persons; had attracted about fifteen-hundred people to a high school gym at the

Valley Christian Center in Dublin. And he had made news headlines by appearing on the same stage with Charles Colson at the National Religious Broadcasters' annual convention in Washington. They were a highly remarkable pair, considering that Colson had been in the Nixon White House during the days when federal operations against black radical groups like the Black Panthers heated up. Two former opponents, experiencing the same "conversion" by the same God in Christ at two different times a continent apart geographically and poles apart politically. Eldridge's "new era" was bringing some startling contrasts.

Public opinion contrasted sharply, also. T.D. Allman listed numerous examples in *The New York Times Magazine* January 16, 1977:

"Reports of Cleaver's political and religious conversion generate strong reactions. Many on the left believe that he has made a cynical and calculated deal with the FBI to gain safe passage back to American life. Elaine Brown, now acting head of the Black Panther Party, has denounced him as 'an active and willing agent in the FBI's COINTELPRO plan to destroy black organizations.' A black newspaper has ridiculed him as a 'Patty Hearst in reverse.' Paul Jacobs, a San Francisco writer who contributed to the bail Cleaver forfeited when he left America in 1968, now dismisses Cleaver as a 'Bicentennial coon.' But Daniel Patrick Moynihan, impressed by Cleaver's denunciations of the Third World, flew to California to confer with him and contributed $500 to his legal defense. Norman Podhoretz, the editor of *Commentary*, held a fund-raising cocktail party for Cleaver, as Felicia and Leonard Bernstein once did for the Black Panthers. . . .

" 'I cannot help wondering,' says one former San Francisco friend. 'Is this just one more of Eldridge's gigantic put-ons, another amazing maneuver?' A black activist, after hearing Cleaver speak, said, 'It's all very obvious. Eldridge got his kicks in the '60s by scaring Whitey. Now he's out to win his freedom by saying just what the Man wants to hear.' He added: 'I can't blame a man for looking out for himself. But this is so transparent.' "

Allman also wrote that "Elsa Knight Thompson, a broadcaster who has reported on Cleaver's activities for more than 10 years, points out that 'Eldridge always has been the salesman par excellence. Maybe he just doesn't care what he's selling. . . .' " And Allman noted that "one estranged member of the Black Panthers remarks that . . . 'The notion that Eldridge *suddenly* has become a turncoat opportunist is absurd. That boy's been running through other people's ideas and other people's money since puberty.' "

Although he wrote that "others go so far as to suggest that Cleaver is losing his mental balance," Allman himself noted in the same *New York Times* piece: ". . . to an interviewer who spends many hours with him, Cleaver comes across as a balanced and lucid man with a strong sense of humor. At the same time, however, he does reveal himself as out of touch with the American reality of today and the reality of the world he traversed between 1968 and 1976. As he travels across America, Cleaver demonstrates a flair for presentation, but he appears to lack a basic understanding of his audiences."

Thus Allman expressed the skepticism and the ambivalent feeling many still feel towards Eldridge.

The observations echo that W. Somerset Maugham wrote long ago: "The most consistent thing about human beings is their inconsistency." Eldridge appears to be inconsistent; he is going against the currents of his former revolutionary thoughts and friends. He is a "turncoat" in a kind of perverse sense—in that he is accused of being a traitor *because* of his new patriotism and belief in the American system. Jesus Christ's words also echo: "A prophet is not without honor save in his own country. . . ."

However, Eldridge is not inconsistent with his own inner passion for truth, for pitting the reality against the dream. Are there different realities? Eldridge's now is that expressed by the apostles and their Lord Jesus Christ. That Eldridge fought and fled and exiled himself and fell, finally, into groveling despair, to wrestle with his conscience and the message of that Mediterranean moon—that is not being inconsistent, in Eldridge's mind. It is absolutely consistent with his lifelong search for the truth of things, of people and of Life itself.

Apparently there are many who agree with this new image, who find in Eldridge this kind of consistency, this stability, who see the "balanced and lucid" man which Allman noticed. In February, 1977, a fund-raising barbecue was held for him in, of all places, Orange County, California, the nesting place of right-wing conservatism, and guests contributed $16,500 to his defense fund.

So, the kind of new man seen depends on whose reality and where the observer stands. The Christian audiences to whom Eldridge speaks feel he has a sure understanding of them and the world as seen through an evangelical Christian's eyes. Everywhere in churches as he finishes speaking, audiences rise to give him a standing ovation and then sit down to dry damp eyes. These people know where Eldridge Cleaver is coming from. They're coming from the same place.

* * * *

Regardless of how suspect one's motives may appear to some people, in the final analysis—until time either confirms or denies him—you have to take a man at face value. Everything else is sheer guesswork. And suspicions arise from envy in those harboring them as often as they do from motives truly warranting such suspicions.

Although thousands of people have heard Eldridge's Christian testimony, at no place did he put himself at the mercy of his audience more than at a Christian writers' press conference in California in January, 1977. Questioning there about his avowed Christianity was as heavy as that on "Meet The Press" had been about his new politics.

Paraphrased, Eldridge told reporters in that ninety-minute session that his remarkable pilgrimage amounted to his making a complete circle in his life. "Finally exhausting all of the false gods and false doctrines and false directions," he said, after straying and going "down a thousand blind alleys" in a long and painful process, he finally returned to truths he'd learned as a child at home. At last he was forced to fall down on his knees and turn his life over to Christ.

"I am in awe of Jesus," he told reporters, "and there are times when I'm just really afraid when I think of how close I came to missing my salvation." His life as a revolutionary had led him to alienate himself from people, but now he sees Jesus as "the bridge between people and God, and between people also."

Ironically, this Christ-ward trail very nearly led to the destruction of his marriage. There was a time when he thought "the Lord would come between myself and my wife." However, he and Kathleen had been through too much together for that, nor was that Christ's purpose for them. So, "I'm very happy to say that we're now companions in the Lord." Eldridge and Kathleen were baptized together in October, 1976, and their two children are now in a Christian school in California.

What kind of future does Eldridge the Christian see for himself? He feels that "in a way, you can say all my time will be invested for Christ." He is interested, first of all, in sharing Christ with people from his past. He will deal primarily with his own subcultural group. His primary vocation, he told reporters, is as a writer, and he wants to finish a lot of partially completed manuscripts strung all over from California to France.

"But I want to devote particularly the next five years to just studying the Gospel . . ." and ". . . translating all the stuff that I've got already in my computer into a new language. . . ."

* * * *

Thus, if you listen long enough, or go over the stories and tape manuscripts thoroughly, you find several recurring themes in Eldridge's new talk: the disillusionment with Marxism and totalitarian dictatorships . . . his not being able to find "a single person that I don't love [the single most important sign to him of his transformed inward state] . . ." and that he returned to the United States "just on faith that I will have a fair day in court, you know?"

As for that day in court, Eldridge didn't ask for a "perfect trial." He said, "I mean just a fair one where the district attorney puts forth his evidence and we put forth our argument and evidence and a jury makes the decision."

To other reporters in later interviews he expanded on his trial outlook. If the Lord wanted him to go to prison, that he loses his case, "then I will go to prison and whatever happens there will happen there."

So, was Eldridge, out on bail and facing trial, really free at last? In one sense he was free until trial time, but after that, what? Yes, he would still be free, trusting that whatever happens will be his Lord's will.

Knowing how Eldridge has ruffled the pages of his Bible till the binding is threading loose, I know he has read Christ's words in the Gospel of John, as that apostle journalist recorded them: "If the Son therefore shall make you free, you shall be free indeed . . . and you shall know the truth and the truth shall make you free. . . ."

Wherever he will ever be, Eldridge Cleaver, reborn, will be a free man.

EPILOGUE

That's not all of the Eldridge Cleaver story.

Humans, being what they are, forever wanting to know why people do what they do, the public keeps old questions alive and raises additional ones as new events leapfrog over old.

For instance, on February 16, 1977, the Reverend Robert Schuller of the Garden Grove Community Church of California, whose "Hour of Power" program is televised weekly to more than 150 stations in the United States, Canada and Australia, wrote California Governor Edmund G. Brown, Jr., asking that Eldridge be granted a pardon. And the February 18, 1977, issue of *Christianity Today* magazine editorialized in the same vein.

Dr. Schuller observed that the Eldridge now facing trial is not the same Eldridge of 1968. "Unquestionably," he wrote Governor Brown, "he is a new . . . and . . . different person. . . ." *Christianity Today* suggested that because of the drastically changed circumstances, perhaps the prosecution should drop the charges or the governor ". . . should . . . issue a pardon. . . . We see in Eldridge Cleaver a repentant man who now intends to devote his life to serving the best interests of the nation. . . ."

This news surprised many who felt that a pardon would surround Eldridge with the same stigma that still overshadows former President Nixon because of his pardon by ex-President Ford. And it makes Eldridge suspect on new grounds. Not only is there suspicion about his changed politics, or skepticism about his announced conversion to Christianity, but now: Is Eldridge using God, in trying to escape going to trial? Is *this* what's *really* behind all his *newthink* and *newtalk*?

Almost forgotten are Eldridge's statements that he returned from exile to have his day in court and that all he asks for is a "fair trial, not a perfect one, just a fair one."

Even though Governor Brown has since replied to Dr. Schuller that he cannot grant a pardon to a man who has not been convicted, public skepticism remains, and people still ask: Where *is* Eldridge coming from anyway? What's the *real* truth behind all he's doing?

* * * *

Only time will tell, but one somehow can't escape the feeling of a lingering familiarity with the Cleaver story, and perhaps the questions can't be answered until we examine this *deja vu* quality, the sights and sounds of other times that tumble down the years. Recognizing them, a person finds himself turning the whole Cleaver affair upside down.

Instead of God being part of Eldridge's story, *Eldridge becomes part of God's story*. And the fragments of history floating by begin to fall into more permanent coherence.

From God's story: I am the only God and there is none other. . . . This is my only Son, hear ye Him. . . . Herein is love—that I first loved you. . . . How many would die for a righteous man, let alone a guilty one? . . . Unless a man is born again, he cannot see the kingdom of God. . . . If any man be in Christ, he is a new creation. . . .

Listening carefully, one can hear the tellers of the tale—Moses, the shepherd king of Israel, the prophet Isaiah, the Big Fisherman, the apostle Paul. Sounding through the centuries, the voices speak in our own times, the words louder now— from "born-again" Charles Colson; from an American president newly moved into the Oval Office from Georgia; from countless others—the famous, the infamous, the unknown. And from Eldridge Cleaver: ". . . I am in awe of Christ. I haven't met anyone that I don't love. . . ." Similarity. Familiarity.

Deja vu. No wonder. The sights and sounds come from the same old gospel story we've heard a million times. God's story. The best seller of all time. If a man can't believe that he can't believe Eldridge.

In God's chapter on Eldridge the story is dressed up in the twentieth century clothes of Eldridge's own times. The Hound of Heaven is seen pursuing a black kid from the ghetto side of society into black manhood in white America, into prison and beyond, through revolutionary rage into isolated exile, and finally back home, into and out of jail again to speak a new

283

language. . . .

In God's story men are full of imperfections, and often stumble in their faith. Eldridge is as human as any and may well trip at some time in the future. When he does, the critical will undoubtedly hurry to shake fingers. But this also is part of God's story.

God never tells *His* story in secret. Though he speaks often in the still, small voice of conscience, He doesn't work in a corner. He throws every detail into public view in order to call attention to Himself: This is *my* story. Pay attention, O ye people. You are *all* parts of it.

That's where Eldridge is coming from: the same place as all of us.

Only the names have been changed. . . .